RUNNING DREAMS

CARLOS R. SERVÁN

RUNNING DREAMS

An Immigrant's hurdles and triumphs,
after blindness and amputation

atmosphere press

I want to dedicate this book to my beloved parents, Honorato and Virginia, who instilled in me strong values.

To all people with disabilities, to who in one way or another strive to compete in a society of high expectations.

To all men and women in the military and law enforcement, who are willing to give their lives to bring peace and protect society.

Chapter One

FOREVER CHANGED

Clutching MP3 automatic rifles, Jesús Sedano and I patrolled the grounds outside the new National Detective Academy during the late afternoon on a chilly day. After four years together as cadets, Jesús had become one of my best friends at the academy, and his presence reassured me as we made our way up the darkening hillside.

We'd arrived at the headquarters—situated on the former Barbadillo Estate—only four days ago. On this day, my first patrol outside the academy walls, I buzzed with adrenaline. Everything I observed in this rural, rough terrain, from birds to cactuses, felt new, fresh, different. I was definitely not in Lima anymore.

We would lift a rock, and a lizard, perfectly camouflaged with its surroundings, would scurry quickly away. Harmless little lizards made us laugh, but the scorpions, the biggest I'd ever seen, commanded respect. We carefully avoided them.

The academy sat like a fortress midway down the northern slope of a large mountain. The running and training we'd done over the past three years made it easier for us to navigate the hilly terrain, but we still moved cautiously.

Looking west from the top of the mountain, you could see perpetual smog in the distance; the dark, unhealthy cloud hung over the city of Lima twelve miles away. To the north, Carretera Central, the main arterial highway leading out of Lima into the Andes, wound its way up the mountain. A railway ran parallel about a hundred yards north of the highway. Another hundred yards past that, the tumultuous, muddy Rimac River wove through the valley. All three—the highway, the railway, and the river—could be seen and heard from the top of that mountain, like three serpents constantly in motion.

Several two-man teams patrolled outside every day looking for anything out of place. On this particular day, one team went to the top of the foothills east of the academy to survey the farm country beyond. Another team patrolled the mountain south of the building. Jesús and I made our way across the lower slopes, below the second team but above the academy. The rough, steep slopes forced us to scramble over the rocks on occasion. Mud and dust splattered on khaki uniforms.

Despite the rough terrain, I felt confident, even happy. I looked forward to the weekend when I could be with my girlfriend, Mary, and my family again. Jesús and I talked a lot about life at the academy. We wondered, too, where we would be assigned after graduation and what fieldwork would be like.

"I want to work for the antiterrorist division, but I understand you don't have a life there," I said. "If you have a girlfriend, the terrorists will try to kill her, so you cannot take her to public places. The same is true if you want to start a family." I also knew the antiterrorist division required long hours, but I still dreamed of helping my country fight terrorism, no matter the cost.

Our commanders warned us to look carefully for signs of Shining Path, a brutal terrorist organization dedicated to communism and the violent overthrow of the government. I fervently longed to fight on the front lines, battling the mindless chaos and misery spread by terrorists.

From the top of the foothills, we looked down on farms and peasants going about their work. The scene seemed peaceful and innocent. But we'd been trained to be aware— any of them might be terrorists. We had no way of knowing because Shining Path routinely struck without warning, inflicted maximum damage, and vanished like smoke into thin air. They kept themselves invisible. They could be anyone. They could be anywhere.

We could also see the obstacle course where upperclass-men and officers shouted vulgarities at first-year cadets in training, goading them to move faster. The sight reminded us of our own first year in the academy. The testing, like nothing we'd experienced before, seemed like it would never end.

All my life, I had been a runner. My mama said I started running as soon as I could stand on two feet. I loved the feeling of strength and freedom that running gave me. And building my endurance and fitness had helped me achieve my goal of attending the academy in the first place. The continued challenges of my training at the academy could shape me into the kind of man I wanted to be.

As we walked, Jesús pointed to some peasants down the hill from us. One woman prepared a cooking fire while another woman and young girl slaughtered a chicken—or at least, tried to do so. The girl did her best to hold down the chicken, as the woman used one hand to position its head for the *coup de grâce,* and the other hand came down with the knife, not quite severing the head. We couldn't hear everything being said, but we could see the girl, maybe ten years old, struggling mightily. The other woman yelled for her to hold on, but it was clearly more than she could handle. The chicken got loose and ran around crazily—its head half cut off, spraying blood over everyone including the woman making the fire. The two women laughed as the girl covered her face with her hands to avoid the spraying blood. We could see a bowl positioned to catch the blood after decapitation, probably to be fried later with onions and tomatoes.

"I don't think they will eat *sangrecita* (fried chicken blood) for supper," Jesús said, laughing.

The scene provided a welcome distraction from our mission, from the dangers that could be anywhere around us. A few weeks before, in the foothills overlooking an affluent community with private clubs, golf courses, swimming pools, soccer fields, and attractive homes just a few miles away, Shining Path erected a large structure depicting the hammer and sickle of the Communist Party. When lit, the structure glowed ominously after dark—no doubt an extraordinarily effective scheme, which struck fear in the minds of all who saw it. In the confrontation that followed, the terrorists fled from the military police and went in different directions over the hills, leaving explosive booby traps behind. Jesús and I had been warned that explosives might be hidden here, so we trod carefully.

The sun dipped toward the horizon as the skies darkened with advancing twilight. We could see mist forming in front of our faces as we breathed the chilly air.

We approached brick ovens, commandeered to burn tons of confiscated cocaine after a recent sting operation. As we moved to investigate some bushes near the ovens, Jesús lowered his voice, although no one was around to hear.

"I wonder if the rumors we heard are true. Do you think some of the policemen who confiscated the cocaine stole some kilos for themselves?" I answered, "Yes, I wonder about it too." Such corruption disgusted us. Evidence of evil confronted us at every turn, and we wanted to do something to fight it, but we also knew that corruption entangled everyone and everything. Though equally frustrated, I felt proud that I was fighting for democracy.

My right boot brushed up against something. The object, about the size of my fist, felt different somehow, lighter than I would have thought for a rock. I picked it up. Its mud-encrusted, rusty surface looked as if it had been shot through by bullets. Suddenly, it exploded in my right hand.

BRIEF HISTORY OF PERU

When Peru was conquered, the Spanish crown granted the right to govern parcels of land in the New World to individuals. Indians living on this land were obligated to work the land and provide the fruits of their labor to the grant holder in return for instruction in the Christian faith and protection from warring tribes. This was called *encomienda*, a feudal arrangement obligating Indians and their descendants to work the land in perpetuity. This also brought a systematic way of corruption from the conquistadores.

Once Peru became independent in 1821, *encomiendas* evolved into large estates called *haciendas*. The lives of native workers improved, but they were still expected to work the land all their lives. The landowners, or *gamonales,* owned the land and often held the highest positions in the government, which also carried more and more corruption. *Gamonalismo* was common practice in Peru, until 1968, when dictator General Velasco brought about land reform, breaking up large *haciendas* and redistributing land through co-ops to the formerly landless workers.

General Juan Velasco became Peru's president after a 1968 coup d'état overthrew Fernando Belaúnde, who had been democratically elected. General Velasco implemented socialist reforms which were supported by the Soviet Union as part of the Cold War.

During the mid and late seventies, several national strikes took place to protest the military government. The military government declared a State of Emergency and implemented martial law, including a national curfew by 5:00 p.m. The television news broadcasted images of people killed at public demonstrations; all across the country, people rioted, neighborhoods burned, and stores were looted. It was chaos. People demanded a return to democracy. Military helicopters fired on crowds of civilians.

The military controlled everything at the national, provincial, and local levels. Most food was subsidized, and everyday necessities were rationed. We were often without water for several days at a time, and when the water was off, we had to walk several blocks with our buckets to wait for water trucks sent to designated locations by the military. With limited access to water, we learned to conserve. We couldn't shower as often as we would have liked, so we took sponge baths. Furthermore, stores were often without basic food items. Even when commodities were available, buying was restricted. It was normal to wait several hours in long lines for water and groceries. Even the lines at banks were long. Fights sometimes broke out between people desperate to get groceries before supplies ran out. It was the normal way of things then.

In October 1975, General Francisco Morales-Bermúdez

overthrew General Velasco, which was supported by the United States, and he reversed many of Velasco's socialist policies. But for everyday people, not much had changed. The lines at grocery stores, water trucks, banks, and so on, were just as long. Furthermore, inflation worsened, corruption increased, unemployment rose, and the pervasive sense of despair deepened. Many people, especially younger people, left Peru for the promise of something better in countries like Venezuela and the United States. Thus, more national strikes asking for democracy were called, shutting down public schools, public services, and hospitals, and blocking several main avenues to stop anybody from working.

In 1978, the military dictatorship oversaw Peru's return to democracy, holding national elections. While Peru was preparing for a democratic national election in early 1980, a new ultra-left group, the Peruvian Communist Party—Shining Path—was growing in influence. It opposed democratic elections, charged the entire political system with corruption, and called for revolution. Shining Path was a Maoist, Marxist, and Leninist organization, otherwise known as *Pensamiento Gonzalo* (Gonzalo Thoughts). "Gonzalo" was the pseudonym for Abimael Guzmán, a philosophy professor in Ayacucho, the founder and president of Shining Path, and the most wanted man by the Peruvian police and military in the 1980s and early '90s.

Corruption was everywhere and at every level, and Shining Path used the government dysfunction to recruit people to its cause, especially idealistic young college students. Fernando Belaúnde won election to a five-year term as president of Peru, taking office on July 28, 1980. Belaúnde had been president of Peru once before, until 1968, before his government was overthrown in a military coup d'état led by General Juan Velasco. After twelve years, Peru's military dictatorship was finally over. However, around the same time,

Shining Path started its terrorist attacks in the most rural areas of the Andes. Terrorists blew up public buildings, police stations, and electric towers, and they assassinated peasants and members of the police and army forces. Most public officials and a good number of citizens in Lima really did not care much about what happened in places like the most rural areas of Peru.

It would become evident that Shining Path had no fear of deploying whatever methods were necessary, no matter how violent, to achieve its objectives.

The reaction of the army and the Civil Guard was terrifying, too. Some of the soldiers and policemen special forces killed groups of innocent peasants because they would not, or could not, provide information about Shining Path. These were extremely hard times for most peasants. If they didn't join or do what Shining Path said, they were in danger of being killed. To escape the growing violence and terrorism raging across the country, many peasants moved from rural regions to Lima. Terror provoked more terror, despair, and violence. It was all the more horrible because no one knew who belonged to Shining Path. The terrorists were always on the move, unpredictable, striking when least expected. Here today, gone tomorrow. Shining Path was the unseen enemy. It was like fighting a ghost, and that mysterious, elusive quality only intensified the terror people felt. The military and police had no coherent strategy for subduing Shining Path.

Terrorist attacks started to move to several large cities in the country, including Lima. To add to the problem, a new terrorist movement was created, Movimiento Revolucionario Tupac Amaru—MRTA—Tupac Amaru Revolutionary Movement. Each time Shining Path declared a general strike in Peru, no one was allowed to go to school or work or to conduct any business with the government. Explosives were detonated in the main squares and large markets in the downtown sections of many cities and towns. Pamphlets calling for revolution and denouncing the imperialist capitalist government were widely distributed.

Shining Path and MRTA called for more general strikes across the country. When the people didn't comply, they retaliated by blocking roads and throwing Molotov cocktails into crowded buses, burning the vehicles and the people inside them. Shining Path also detonated car bombs made from dynamite stolen from mining operations in the Andes, taking more lives and destroying government buildings. Public alarm and fear ran high. The violent attacks appeared random. The politicians, military leaders, and police looked inept, unable to anticipate when or where the next attack would come from.

With violence erupting in the nation's capital, officials in Lima (especially the military, police, and politicians) became alarmed enough to take stronger offensive measures against Shining Path. The Policia de Investigaciones del Peru (Peruvian Investigation Police) created a Direccion Contra el Terrorismo (National Antiterrorist Division commonly known as DIRCOTE). This was a clear indication that the government was finally taking the terrorist organizations seriously.

In 1985, Alan Garcia was elected president, but things didn't get better. Peru's economic, political, and social conditions continued to decline. Shining Path and MRTA became even stronger. Terrorism was still a threat and spreading. The political unrest frustrated efforts by the national government to attract foreign investors. The economy floundered. People from the Andes were still moving to Lima in large numbers to escape poverty and violence, and the number of people leaving Peru to immigrate to other countries steadily increased. Peru became a hostile country, where people lived in a state of constant terror and mistrust, and vigilance became the center of everyone's existence.

Chapter Two

THE WEDDING NEXT DOOR

Mama, Papa, and my three older siblings lived on the north side of Lima in Pampa de Cueva (Desert of the Caves), a dusty shantytown with no streets, no sidewalks, and no indoor plumbing. On February 5, 1966, a hot summer day, I was born at the Police Hospital in Lima. It would be another three years before my family could afford to move to a better neighborhood with indoor plumbing. In 1969, we moved to the south side of Lima in the district of San Juan de Miraflores (San Juan for short), the neighborhood where I grew up.

From the time I could walk, my family remembers me being in constant motion: running, climbing walls, playing hard. I wore out my shoes—when I had shoes—faster than my parents could afford to buy new ones, so they got me llanques (pronounced Yankees), sandals fashioned from tire rubber. Also called *huaraches*, they're popular because they are inexpensive and last a long time.

I wore my brother's hand-me-downs, which, of course, did not fit me. Mama simply shortened the pant legs, and I used a thin rope to keep my pants tight around my waist. Later, Mama learned to adjust the pants to fit me by taking in the back seam.

"You should not be embarrassed about being poor," Papa told us. "Always walk with your shoulders straight and head up. People who are lazy or steal from others should be embarrassed, but there is nothing wrong with being poor and working hard to improve your life."

When I was three, we lived in a shack made out of reeds and cardboard boxes. By the time I had turned four, my Papa had added a kitchen and then a dining room made of bricks, where we all slept. Finally, he added the bathroom, a separate structure made of reeds and cardboard balanced on four brick walls to form a roof. It took about a year to build. Eventually, we replaced the cardboard and reeds with a corrugated plastic roof. Two or three years later, the garage and the living room, made also of bricks, were added, each of them with a door to the street. Now, the boys slept in the garage and the girls and parents in the dining room. The living room was used as a dining room and area for the children to play.

By the time I was seven, my older brother, sisters, and I all had our daily assigned chores. We cleaned the backyard, front yard, dining and living areas, bathroom, and windows. I was assigned to clean the bathroom every day, including the tiles— a task I typically finished right after breakfast.

The neighborhood grew slowly. During summer break from school, I would finish my chores, then go down the street to play with my friend, Juan Jimenez. One day, I sat on the sidewalk waiting for Juan, and I noticed ten wire baskets on the sidewalk, each with twelve bottles of milk. A delivery truck deposited the milk there for Mr. Borges, the local milkman, to deliver to our neighbors.

A dog came by and started sniffing the milk bottles. I picked up a stick and waved it over my head to scare the dog away. Just then, Mr. Borges happened by and saw me protecting the milk. He thanked me and gave me five centavos. He promised to pay me five centavos every day if I would keep dogs away until he picked up the milk. I had started my first job!

After a week or so, Mr. Borges asked me if I would like to help him with his deliveries in other neighborhoods—a promotion! Excited, I ran off to tell Papa, but he already knew about it. Mr. Borges had talked to him before offering me the job.

Papa addressed me seriously, "Listen, hijo (son), you don't have to work. You have food, clothes, and a roof over your head. But if you want to work for Mr. Borges, you will learn how to work and save money, and that will be a good thing."

I enjoyed helping Mr. Borges, a kind, hard-working man. Mr. Borges used a freight tricycle to make his daily delivery. Metal baskets fit neatly into an open, foot-high cargo box mounted on two front wheels. And once he hired me, he simply tucked me, his small-framed, seven-year-old assistant, into the front of that open box. He pedaled us from house to house. I stayed with the tricycle while he carried the milk bottles to each house. I helped occasionally, delivering single bottles to homes near the road. Usually, Mr. Borges left two or three bottles of milk on the front door mat. The *panadero* (bread man) would later deliver bread, tying a plastic bag of breakfast rolls on the front door handle. They don't do that anymore, as the bread is sure to be stolen.

Sometimes, dogs guarding the house where we needed to make a delivery came after us, intent on biting us. Mr. Borges showed me how to protect myself using an empty metal basket held like a shield. The dogs would try to get around the basket, but I always kept the basket between me and the dogs. I felt like the lion tamer in the circus. It may sound dangerous, but it thrilled me. I learned to not be afraid of dogs.

After delivering the milk, we ate breakfast in the southeast part of town where the residential area ended, near the minibus terminal. After breakfast, we went back to each house to collect the empty bottles and money for the milk. We tapped an empty milk bottle with a small stone to make a loud clinking sound and yelled, *"La leche! La leche!"* ("The milk! The milk!")

Housewives brought out the empty bottles and paid Mr. Borges while I took the empty bottles back to the three-wheeler. Mr. Borges handled all the money. I just delivered and brought back the bottles. I worked for Mr. Borges for a couple of years during summer breaks and weekends during the school year. My job ended when bakeries started selling bags of milk (like juice pouches kids drink after sporting events but large enough to hold a liter of milk). That change of events made me wonder what I would do when I grew up!

In my earliest memories of Mama, she was always busy doing chores. She would wrap my baby sister, Vicky, in a thick blanket and tie the blanket around her neck to hold Vicky on her back. With a baby on her back, Mama cleaned the house, hand washed the clothes, ironed, and cooked for our family of seven. She always had lunch ready as soon as my brother and sisters returned home from school.

Though she had only a third-grade education, she always exhibited patience, kindness, gentleness—the fruits of the Spirit in her life. She taught us sound moral values and made herself available to us consistently. She showed us to always have faith in God.

Mama also worked outside the home to bolster our family's income. She learned to crochet so she could make and sell baby clothes, shawls, and scarves. She also sewed and repaired clothes and cut neighbors' hair—all to help make ends meet.

Papa served as a sergeant in the Guardia Republicana (Republican Guard), a steady job that kept a roof over our heads—even though that roof sometimes leaked. A very strict, hard-working, persevering, and responsible man, he expected his children to do their best at all times. Papa's parents, peasant farmers, worked all day every day and raised him to do the same. Consequently, he grew up believing "There is always something to do." He told us so whenever we had finished our chores.

My parents created a solid, supportive home environment; they instilled in us the importance of being modest, hard-working, and respectful of others.

* * * *

One day, when I was about eight years old, I saw an envelope on the table. It contained an invitation to a wedding and reception to be held next door. I read the address: Mr. Honorato Serván and Family. The "and family" caught my attention right away. It meant that the invitation included the children! The idea of attending thrilled me. I had never attended a wedding reception before. In fact, I had never attended a party or celebration of any kind except for one or two children's birthday parties.

The wedding was going to take place in about two weeks. As far as I was concerned, it couldn't come soon enough. The prospect of dancing to lively music, eating delicious food, and meeting new people excited me to my core! I could think of little else.

Finally, the day of the big event came. As soon as I got up that morning, I peppered Mama with questions. "When are we going to the wedding?"

"We'll go when Papa gets home." Mama shooed me away as she went about preparing breakfast for the family.

Papa wouldn't get home until later in the day, sometime near evening. I counted the hours until the reception. Mama seemed weirdly calm and relaxed with such an exciting event about to happen. She did not seem to be looking forward to the party all that much. No one else in my family appeared to care or even notice either. None of my brothers and sisters prepared by cleaning their shoes, ironing their clothes, or doing anything else to get ready. I thought it was strange but decided to not worry about it. Mama had said we'd go when Papa came home, and that was good enough for me.

The invitation said that women should wear dresses, and men should wear jackets and ties. I didn't have a suit, but I did have my school uniform—a pair of gray shorts, a white button-down shirt, and gray socks—all of it three sizes too large because it had been handed down from my brother, Edgar. I also had a blue jacket from Edgar's first communion, also three sizes too big. For shoes, I had only my llanques.

After I found the wedding reception invitation, Papa gave me a tie and taught me how to tie it. "There are several ways to tie a tie," he said as he demonstrated different styles, "and the one that looks best is the one that takes the most time. You see, hijo, if you don't take the time to tie a really good-looking tie, you will get in the habit of settling for good enough. Then, if you take the same attitude with cleaning your room, doing your homework, or doing anything else, you end up living a lazy lifestyle. You wind up always being second rate and never looking or doing your best. If you find a job, you won't be promoted. You might even get fired."

He looked deep into my eyes to impress on me the gravity of his words. "It is important to develop good habits early in life," he said. "As you grow older, these habits become part of your life. You will be known as a hard worker who always does his best. People will notice and will enjoy working with you."

I looked over the different knots that Papa had tied, and I

agreed. The best-looking one required the most time and attention. Then Papa untied the tie and handed it to me, telling me to knot the tie myself. I felt uncertain, but Papa told me to try. I gave it my best and was surprised when I found I was able to tie it the way Papa had, although it took me far longer. Though I was happy with the result, I must have looked downcast because of how long it had taken me to tie the tie.

Papa said, "With practice, it will become easier, hijo."

The day before the reception, Mama had washed our school uniforms and hung them out to dry on the clothesline in our small backyard. I ran back often to check whether my clothes had dried so I could iron them. My shirt and socks dried quickly, but my pants needed more time. By late afternoon, all my clothes had dried. In Lima, there is seldom more than a slight breeze, so people just drape their laundry over the clothesline instead of using clothespins. I had to jump to get them down.

I was naturally curious and took a keen interest in the things Papa and Mama did around the house. Mama always took the time to answer our questions about household activities, knowing that we had to learn how to take care of ourselves.

"What is that little dial on the iron for?" I had asked as I watched her.

"The dial adjusts the temperature, depending on the type of material. For shirts, you turn the dial halfway," she explained. "For pants, you need to turn it three-quarters of the way, but you need to place newspaper on top of the pants when you iron them, otherwise they become shiny and don't look nice. You also need to sprinkle a little water on the pants when you iron them."

As the time for the reception drew closer, I followed Mama around the house. "Are you going to iron our clothes?" I asked. Why wasn't she doing more to get ready for the wedding reception? She didn't answer my question; I'm not sure she heard me. She seemed more focused on knitting baby clothing to sell. Maybe she was thinking about some unpaid bills. She turned her attention to making dinner. I didn't want to bother her anymore.

I decided to iron my own clothes. I got out the ironing board—no easy feat for me. Each time Mama finished ironing, she left the ironing board standing and pushed it out of the way rather than folding it up. I managed to drag the ironing board out to the middle of the room, but I couldn't lower it to a more comfortable level. Though the ironing board came up to my chest, I still made it work.

The iron was heavy and a bit awkward. I remembered Mama moved the iron back and forth over the clothes just like a toy car, so that's what I did. I started with my shirt. I liked the way the fabric transformed from wrinkled to smooth. I hung the shirt over the back of a chair. Then, I adjusted the dial to a hotter temperature for the pants. I sprinkled some water on the pants, spread newspaper over them, and started to iron, just the way Mama taught me. The pants looked professional, in my opinion. I knew then that I liked to iron.

I laid the clothes out on my bed so they wouldn't get wrinkled. I made sure that Papa's tie was properly tied and ready to go. Then I polished my llanques. I was ecstatic with the results. They had been absolutely transformed, in my eyes, and they looked great, almost new!

Then I took a cold shower (we didn't have a hot-water heater) using laundry soap. I even washed my hair with the laundry detergent, since we couldn't afford body soap or shampoo.

My feet swam in oversized socks—the only ones I owned. Empty sock material stuck out past my toes. I folded the ends of my socks back under my toes to hide the excess material. So long as I didn't run around too much, maybe no one would notice.

The sleeves on Edgar's blue jacket hung down to my knees. No problem. When I put it on, I just folded the sleeves back up under until my hands showed. My clothes had a distinct hand-me-down appearance, but I didn't feel especially self-conscious. Mama and Papa had taught us not to feel bad because we couldn't afford to have everything we wanted. They taught us to wear clean clothes, treat others well, and walk with our shoulders straight and our heads held high. Actually, once I had dressed and combed my hair with cooking oil to give it a glossy sheen, I thought I looked pretty darned good!

As the sun set, I ran outside to check on developments next door. The guests started to arrive. I relished the warm, clear night, as I glanced up at the bright shining stars. I heard people say that the bride and groom were on their way. A few minutes later, the couple arrived. The beautiful bride in her long white dress looked radiant as she stepped out of a black car. The handsome groom came around and took her arm. Together they walked to the house through a shower of rice.

Papa was not home yet, Mama continued her sewing, and my brothers and sisters seemed oblivious. I couldn't understand what was wrong with everyone. The family honor was at stake. I had to do something! I ran back home by the garage door to grab Edgar's jacket and the invitation card. Taking one last look at myself in the small mirror in the bathroom, I felt satisfied that I looked at least as nice as the other wedding guests—dark suit jacket, tie, and white shirt, as specified in the invitation. No one else wore llanques, though.

At the door, a greeter checked invitation cards as guests arrived. He allowed people wearing the proper attire into the house. When I presented my invitation card, the greeter looked skeptical. He surveyed my well-combed shiny hair, my neat clothes, and my polished llanques. Then he smiled with a mixture of approval and amusement and let me enter.

I wasted no time going around introducing myself to

everyone in the living and dining rooms. I even introduced myself to the women in the kitchen. No children my age attended, which I thought was odd. Some of the women smiled and asked me where I lived. When I said that I lived next door, one woman asked about my parents. "Mama is waiting for Papa to get home from work," I said. Everyone I met treated me with kindness and respect.

A savory, spicy aroma came from the kitchen where the women cooked seco de cordero, a delicious Peruvian lamb stew with yellow potatoes seasoned with aji peppers, cumin, and lots of cilantro served over rice. The lamb is braised in beer until it is tender and flavorful. Aji amarillo, a hot pepper sauce, is served alongside.

I helped pass out plates of seco de cordero, since I had been taught to wait for seniors to eat first. After I ate, I danced with several women. All the men took turns dancing with the bride, starting from the oldest to the youngest. As the youngest one there, I was the last one to dance with the bride. She didn't seem to mind that I was about half her height.

The band played salsa and Afro-Peruvian music, and I got into the spirit of the occasion. I danced up a storm, spinning and shaking all over the dance floor. I thoroughly enjoyed myself!

I had been at the reception for about three hours when the band took a break. The guests relaxed, sitting and talking. From where I sat in the dining room, I could see into the living room and out the open front door to the small fence outside by the sidewalk. To my surprise, Mama stood out there, peering in. I waved at her. She squinted her eyes, looking back, not entirely sure that I was the one waving at her. Finally, she beckoned for me to come over. She did not look happy.

"Mama, why didn't you come to the party?" I asked as I came up to her at the fence.

She answered with a question of her own. "Where did you

get those clothes?"

Upon closer inspection, she recognized my uniform, Edgar's jacket, and my llanques. Her face set in a frown, she told me to go home. On the way back, I could see that the ends of my socks had come loose. I hadn't run, but I had danced quite a bit. When I arrived at our house, I saw that Papa still hadn't come home.

I later learned that Mama and Papa never planned on attending the wedding reception. They didn't have the right clothes. They just didn't have the heart to tell me. But I had no regrets about the evening. I had fun, ate good food, danced, and, most importantly, I had represented the Serván family. It was a great experience!

Chapter Three

TERROR IN AYACUCHO

Peru did not have a law enforcement institution when it became independent in the early nineteenth century, just the army. To deal with crime back then, the Guardia Republicana was created out of the army, a kind of National Guard. Eventually, the Guardia Civil was also created to patrol the streets and prevent crime. In the twentieth century, the Guardia Republicana became responsible for providing security for the Peruvian Department of Corrections, public buildings and public property, and the borders. The Guardia Civil was given police stations to fight minor crimes and the responsibility to control traffic, car accidents, and highway patrol, in addition to patrols on foot, on horses, or in their police cars. As crime evolved and became organized, the Policia de Investigaciones Del Peru (Peruvian Investigation Police) was created "commonly known as detectives". These detectives were the equivalent of the FBI. These three law enforcement entities inherited some of the military training from the army, including their rank officers and noncommissioned officers.

By 1980—when I was fourteen years old—I already wanted very much to follow in my father's footsteps. But, as he would say, "I am a noncommissioned officer, because I finished high school in my mid-twenties and was too old to get into officer school. However, if you want a military or law enforcement career, there is no reason for you not to aim for officer school." He said that with hope and pride in his voice.

In 1980, democracy had been restored after twelve years of military dictatorship. Mayors were also elected, and then construction companies put in their proposals for several projects. As a result, in 1981, my dad got a part-time job with one of these construction companies, coordinating the supplies needed for each new project. This was also the kind of job Dad did in the Guardia Republicana. The extra income from Dad's part-time job helped us a great deal, especially for our clothing and to finish building the second floor at home.

In 1982, I was sixteen years old and already six feet tall. I had a brand-new school uniform for a change—not a hand-me-down from Edgar—and new shoes. I was close to finishing my last year of high school. My classmates and I talked a great deal about what we would do with our lives after graduation. I thought I knew what I was going to do. I was going to fight terrorism—maybe as an officer in the Peruvian Army or one of the police institutions.

One evening in May, Papa sat me down to discuss my future. His face looked serious but not stern. "Carlos, it's time you tell me what you are going to do with your life after you finish school and how you plan to make it happen."

Papa had already had similar conversations with my older brother and two sisters, so I was ready for this. I didn't miss a beat. "I want to enroll in a program that will prepare me for the entrance examination into Officer School for the Army."

Papa was not surprised, in fact, I could see pride in his eyes when he nodded his head. My brother Edgar had already made the same decision. I think it pleased him that I wanted to continue the family tradition. Then he laid out a plan of action. "Hijo, you will need to find out what institute offers the preparatory classes that will best meet your needs. After school tomorrow, come home for lunch. Then head for Lima, and check out those places and find out exactly what they offer and how much they cost."

He reached into his pocket and pulled out some coins. "Here, money for the bus."

I understood the importance of education and the value of hard work because I'd observed my parents my whole life, and Papa was making it clear that the decisions I made now would determine the course the rest of my life was to take. I knew he expected me to make careful, considered, mature choices.

While still in the final year of high school, potential candidates for Officer School for the Army typically enrolled in a preparatory institute that helped them get ready for the entrance examination for higher education. I walked for miles in downtown Lima visiting the institutes that offered training for pre-cadets. I crossed most of them off my list because they were too expensive. I looked over the course curricula and class syllabuses and scrutinized their success rates for graduates getting into officer school. I studied the training protocol that would prepare candidates for the application process, including the physical fitness tests and exercises, the multiple practice academic tests, and the personal interview—the last step in the formal admissions process. After I found the preparatory institute that I thought would best meet my needs, I headed home to report my findings to Papa.

Papa was waiting for me. He listened intently as I told him

what I had learned and why the institute I chose was a good one. I knew he wanted me to feel good about the path I was taking, mindful of the finances involved, and who was paying the bills.

"This is not going to be easy. It will be hard work. Your schedule and training will be demanding. You will need to be mature and self-disciplined. You will have to make a commitment to make this happen."

Papa's eyes bore into mine. He wanted me to understand the gravity of my situation, to be perfectly clear. I knew in both my mind and my heart: You didn't mess with Papa.

Starting in June 1982, my new schedule was as follows:

8:00 a.m.–1:00 p.m.	Attend high school
1:00 p.m.–1:45 p.m.	Eat lunch at home
1:45 p.m.–2:30 p.m.	Ride the bus to downtown Lima
2:30 p.m.–6:00 p.m.	Attend preparatory classes at the institute
6:00 p.m.–8:00 p.m.	Run/get physical exercise
8:00 p.m.–9:00 p.m.	Shower, dress, and go to the bus stop
9:00 p.m.–9:45 p.m.	Ride the bus back to San Juan
9:45 p.m.–10:00 p.m.	Eat dinner
10:00 p.m.–11:30 p.m.	Do homework

The institute prepared us for the full range of psychometric testing administered as part of the application process for admission to officer school, including testing in the areas of career aptitude, academic achievement, overall general knowledge, and cultural awareness. The program also included physical fitness and prepared us for the personal interview, the final step in the application process. Once a month on a weekend, we went to a municipal park about an hour away to engage in physical training, including the 100-meter dash, the 400-meter run, the 1.6-kilometer (1 mile) run, the long jump, pull-ups, the long-distance cross-country run, and so on.

We were expected to practice self-discipline—eat balanced meals, not smoke or consume alcohol, and not stay out late partying. Though I found the training rigorous, I enjoyed the physical activities. I had always been active growing up and especially liked long-distance running. I didn't know how to swim, however, and I knew that would be a challenge.

I allowed myself a break from homework and exercise only on Sunday evenings when I relaxed with friends from the neighborhood. My rigorous schedule typified that of fifth-year high school students planning to go on to higher education.

On the romantic aspect, because now I was one of the tallest boys in the class, I could not help noticing that the girls started to look at me differently, and that boosted my confidence and self-esteem. I especially enjoyed being around Mary, a girl from my neighborhood. Mary walked past our house in the mornings on her way to school. At times, I would stay inside, watching through the curtains, waiting. I would leave the house just as she passed by. I wanted her to think it was just a coincidence. When she saw me, she always smiled, and we walked to school together. From time to time, I looked for her after school so we could walk home together. Occasionally, I looked for her during recess. I liked being around her, but I felt awkward and clumsy. I didn't always know what to say or do. I never worked up enough courage to tell her how I felt. I think Mary knew I liked her, but she didn't say anything to encourage me. She was always nice and seemed to enjoy my company, but I had a hard time figuring out how she felt. She was not being coy. Back then, it would have been unthinkable for a girl to take the initiative or flirt with a boy.

I looked for Mary one day during recess, but she wasn't with her regular friend. I went to the building where she had her classes and found her holding hands with a boy from her class. They were smiling at each other. I was devastated! She didn't see me, thank God. I didn't want her to see me looking so miserable. I was despondent for weeks, just going through the motions. It was especially bad when I saw them holding hands and looking happy as they walked past my house. I suppose it was just part of growing up, but, if the experience were one of life's lessons, it was a very painful one. My confidence and self-esteem went down. I finished the school year with good grades and a broken heart.

● ● ● ●

August is midwinter in Peru, and most days are overcast, cool, and misty. That's the way it was one Sunday night when I started out on a walk in the neighborhood. After just a few blocks, I spotted Teofilo, an old school chum, walking toward me. What a great surprise! I hadn't seen him for a year or so. We met at the corner of a street intersecting the one I lived on. Teofilo was smoking a cigarette as we greeted each other and shook hands. I was really happy to see him again.

Teofilo, now a soldier in the Peruvian Army, was on furlough from Ayacucho, a district in the Andes known to be a stronghold of Shining Path. The army had occupied the area earlier in the year, setting up a red emergency zone. Hundreds of heavily armed soldiers marched in formation while military jeeps sped through the streets. During a TV interview, the general in charge of the emergency mission said, "The Peruvian Army is here to stay until terrorism is completely eliminated. We will protect the people of Ayacucho and keep them safe. Things should be back to normal in another month or two."

Seven months later, things had only gotten worse. People in the region were more terrorized than ever, and there was no indication that Shining Path would be brought under control.

Shining Path splashed slogans in red paint on buildings

across Ayacucho: "The people have ears everywhere," "Death to the dogs who commit treason against the movement," "Beware, traitors, imperialists, and capitalists," and "Long live the armed struggle." The hammer and sickle, symbol of the Communist Party, appeared everywhere.

I told Teofilo about my own plans for a military career. He seemed more confident and mature than when I had seen him last, different somehow from the person I had known before. As we talked, his eyes constantly darted around as if there might be trouble. He said that he would be going back to Ayacucho in a week.

I wanted him to tell me more. "Have you guys caught any terrorists? The TV cameras only show what they want us to see, but you are there and know what is really going on."

Teofilo looked off into the distance as he considered his answer. He said finally, "See, Carlos, we haven't caught anyone." Then he lapsed back into silence, as if not sure what to say next.

"Why not?" For some reason, I felt compelled to press him for more information. "You guys have lots of soldiers and all kinds of weapons. What's the deal?"

Teofilo didn't say anything right away; instead, he gazed at nothing in particular, as if still lost in thought. He took a deep drag of his cigarette, exhaled a cloud of smoke, and finally said, "Carlos, the problem is that we can't tell the regular citizens of Ayacucho from the terrorists. They all dress and act the same. See, we were trained for conventional warfare, to fight against other soldiers, not our own people. We know how to attack the places where the enemy is known to be, but in Ayacucho we don't even know who they are. If we were fighting an army with soldiers wearing uniforms or if we came under attack, it would be different. We would know what to do. Fighting against terrorists is like punching at shadows. They strike and disappear into thin air before we can do anything. Poof. Just like that.

"For instance," he continued, "a few days after we arrived in Ayacucho, we went out to show the people that the army was in town and that peace would be established. An experienced sergeant and a lieutenant led around 200 soldiers in our troop. We came in like we were going to kick ass. Everyone carried automatic rifles and grenades and wore backpacks stuffed with ammunition. No one who could hear our marching boots had any doubt that the army was on its way. We marched into town and turned down a major street, proceeding for ten blocks or so. Then we doubled back the way we came on the opposite side of the street. The streets were all empty and quiet because of the curfew and martial law.

"Spotting something he didn't like on the wall of a dilapidated building ahead of us, the lieutenant gave the signal to ready our rifles. Advancing cautiously, soldiers on the left and right pointed their guns to either side of the formation; those in the rear turned around and walked backwards.

"We were all afraid of what was going to happen next, but we kept moving forward. When we got to the wall that drew the lieutenant's attention, the lights of the town suddenly went out, except for the blocks we were on. We were absolutely terrified. The wall was splashed with red paint, giving the impression that it was blood. Because the town was totally dark, we could make out something in the distance on the middle of the mountain. There, we saw the symbol of the Communist Party, the hammer and sickle, bright and clear. It was as if some invisible force created that symbol, and there was nothing we could do about it. My fellow soldiers and I felt like the air was suddenly sucked free of oxygen, and we were immobilized with fear. The lieutenant and sergeant tried to stay calm, but you could see that they were badly shaken. They had no idea what to do next.

"After that, we looked everywhere—doorways, windows,

alleys—anywhere someone could hide. We didn't see a soul moving anywhere. Then the sergeant spotted a dead dog, with his balls in his mouth, hanging from a light pole. A message splashed on a wall close by in bright red letters warned, 'This is how the dogs who commit treason against the armed struggle will die.' The lieutenant ordered us to keep going and be ready to shoot anything that moved, but the only thing moving was the blood dripping from the dying dog."

Teofilo finished his cigarette and put it out by stepping on the butt. He lit another and took a long drag, exhaling slowly.

"See, Carlos. One moment we thought we were invincible, armed to the teeth, confident in our sergeant and lieutenant. The next moment we feared for our lives like we never had before. I thought I knew what fear was, but I was wrong. This felt like something else entirely. My confidence had evaporated—like it had never been there. Even worse, the terrorists didn't have to shoot a single bullet or do anything. Nothing moved. It was totally silent and mostly dark. We could hear only the sound of our hearts beating fast. That, Carlos, is what we face in Ayacucho, and the army still has no idea how to fight it. How the hell are we supposed to fight those damn terrorists?"

Teofilo paused for a moment to take another drag from his cigarette. I was about to ask another question, but he stopped me with a wave of his hand.

"Wait, Carlos. There's more," he said, looking off into the far distance again as he continued. "We interrogated the peasants for information, anything that would tell us who was responsible for the terrorism. Most were innocent and knew nothing, I'm sure, but if they couldn't tell us anything, our men tortured them until we were satisfied that they were telling the truth.

"After that day, the lieutenant acted as if he was royally pissed off, but I think he was scared shitless. He took thirty of us to a small village near where we saw the hammer and sickle on display on the side of the mountain to search for terrorists. Of course, we saw no obvious terrorists, just hardworking peasants tending their meager fields. He ordered us to round up all the men and line them up in a row. He got the youngest in front and the oldest in back, maybe twelve men in all. He ordered the first one to tell him who and where the terrorists were. The man had no idea, did not want to answer, or was afraid of retaliation. Whatever the case, he said he didn't know. The lieutenant shot him in the head. The guy just dropped dead. The lieutenant moved to the next in line and went through the routine again, eventually going down the entire line, killing them one by one in cold blood. These men were unarmed and scared. Some prayed before they died. Women and children watching nearby wailed pathetically. This sickening scene unfolded right before our eyes! The lieutenant was like a man possessed."

When Teofilo finally came to the end of his story, his face bore a look of deep sorrow. He sniffed and wiped underneath his nose.

I had no idea what had been going on in Ayacucho. I felt sorry for my friend and even sorrier for those poor peasants and their families in the Andes. I had to ask, "Did you find out how they made the sign of the hammer and sickle on the mountainside?"

Again, Teofilo took his time before answering. "It looked so elaborate, but it was actually pretty simple," he said with a little laugh. "They made torches from empty condensed milk cans filled with kerosene and coarse cotton fibers or frayed yarn for wicks. These were lit just before the blackout. They used a lot of those torches to get that damn symbol to look so perfect."

As Teofilo talked, I kept thinking that everything the army did in Ayacucho seemed like a waste of time. Shining Path was only growing more aggressive, attacking more often, going to more places, creating more chaos and death, killing more police and military personnel, assassinating more public officials, and bombing more buildings. They left widespread devastation and wretched conditions wherever they went. More and more people with the means to do so were leaving Peru for Europe or the United States, hoping for a better life. Many left because they knew Shining Path would kill them if they stayed.

Teofilo stopped speaking. A chill ran through my body that had nothing to do with the cool winter air. My friend's terrible story only fortified my resolve to join the army. I wanted to be part of the fight to end terrorism and the violence that had ruined so many lives.

The institute's preparatory training concluded around the same time I graduated from high school, but the entrance examinations for officer school were still six weeks off. I had to continue training as hard as ever to keep in top physical condition if I wanted to be ready for the physical fitness tests, including the 100-meter dash, 1.6-kilometer run, long jump, pull-ups, and swimming—to all be administered the same morning.

I got up at 5:00 every morning and ran about six miles at a six-minute-per-mile pace. Every third day, I ran four miles west to the beach on the Pacific Ocean. After running on the sand as fast as I could for ten minutes, I took my tennis shoes and socks off, got in the water up to my chest, and ran as hard as I could against the water. Then, I practiced swimming, something I had only just learned how to do during my training at the institute.

About seven months earlier, I had installed a metal bar across the space that opened to a third-floor bedroom. That's where I practiced pull-ups. When I started, I could only do two pull-ups at a time, but I gradually improved with practice. By

December, I could do eighteen pull-ups, the maximum required for that portion of the physical examination (the minimum was twelve). I became ever more focused on the rigorous program of study, exercise, diet, and regular sleep that I set for myself as the time for the entrance examinations for officer school came ever closer.

• Chapter Four •

CHRISTMAS EVE, 1982

Early on the morning of Christmas Eve, Mama and I walked about a mile and a half southwest to a dairy farm on a small estate owned by the Catholic Church. The church also operated an orphanage on the estate. The orphans worked on the farm, milking or feeding the cows, carrying water, laying down straw for bedding, cleaning the stalls, and so on. The cows, all of which had names, were very tame and came when called.

We had brought a couple of buckets to fill with milk. Two orphan boys, fourteen or fifteen years old, helped us with our order. As they milked the cows and filled the buckets, Mama made conversation and invited them for Christmas dinner that night. Neither boy said anything or otherwise reacted.

Maybe they got this kind of invitation all the time. Maybe they didn't want people to feel sorry for them. Who knows? As they finished our order, Mama wrote our address on a piece of paper, handed it to the boys, and told them what time to come over if they wanted to join us for Christmas dinner. One of the boys politely took the paper and put it in a pocket without even looking at it. Their business with us concluded, they hurried to serve the next customer. As Mama and I walked home, neither of us said anything about the two orphans. Truth be told, I completely forgot all about them as soon as we left the estate.

Back home, we cleaned and adorned the house with additional Christmas decorations. Over time, we had continued to improve our little home. We'd covered the concrete floor with nicely patterned wooden parquet flooring and trimmed the stairs with wood, including wooden handrails. Simple but pretty curtains hung in the windows. We weren't the same poor family of just two years before when Papa only made just above minimum wage and had to support a family that had grown to eight kids! Edgar now studied at the National Guard Officer School. Both Veronica and Monica had government jobs in the Congressional building, and Papa worked an extra job. We were doing well. God had blessed us.

All day long, we brought presents to the living room and put them under the tree. Each of us—except Ernesto and Gloria—got presents for everybody, making a total of around forty to forty-five presents crowded under the tree. I never imagined that we would ever have a Christmas with so many presents. When I'd been Ernesto's age, we received one present each, usually one piece of clothing that had to last for the whole year. Still, I never remember feeling any lack. Instead, I felt happy that my parents treated all of us with kindness and love.

I helped Papa arrange the Christmas lights around the windows and place the nativity set in the living room under the stairs. Then around 9:45, I went to a neighborhood store just a few houses north of us to get a few last-minute items for dinner. I walked along, enjoying the clear evening and the Christmas lights in our neighbors' windows. On my way home, I spied two silhouetted figures about a block away, walking north toward our house. Who could that be? I took a closer look. I suddenly recognized the two boys from the orphanage! They had to be coming for dinner. Excited, I ran the rest of the way home.

I burst into the kitchen. "Mama, the two orphans are coming! They are almost at the corner."

To my great surprise and consternation, Mama looked worried. I thought she would be happy they had decided to come. I knew we had more than enough food for everyone. What could be the problem?

"Oh, I feel so bad," she fretted. "We have so many presents under the Christmas tree, but there's nothing for them. When they didn't say anything at the farm, I thought they wouldn't be coming. What are we going to do now?"

My brother Enrique, almost thirteen years old, and Papa, putting decorations around the window frame, stopped their work and stared blankly at us. Christmas music could be heard coming in from the living room.

"Maybe there's something in my room for them," I said.

I ran up the stairs to the bedroom I shared with my brothers, taking three steps at a time. Enrique followed right behind me. I saw my most precious belonging, my leather jacket. I only wore the jacket on special occasions, so it looked almost as good as new. I felt a nudge in my spirit, and I knew what I should do. What I wanted to do.

I took down the jacket and folded it neatly. Enrique grabbed his own leather jacket and did the same. Mama and Papa had given him the jacket just a few months before. We looked at each other and smiled, enjoying a moment of brotherly solidarity. Even though the leather jackets were the first items of luxury our parents could afford to give us, we thought they would approve. They had raised us not only to have faith but also to live it out. We wrapped the jackets in gift paper.

We came down the stairs and spotted the two orphans sitting on the sofa. A tape recorder in the living room played Christmas music. The two orphan boys sitting together in this festive place looked like the scene on a perfect Christmas card. They didn't look especially cheery though. When Enrique and I greeted them, they just nodded their heads. They said nothing and kept their expressions carefully neutral, even guarded.

The boys, one a couple of inches taller than the other, wore old but clean clothes and well-worn shoes. They looked freshly showered; their hair was carefully combed. Without saying a word, Enrique and I placed the hastily wrapped presents with the others under the tree. My heart raced with joy and anticipation. Our guests seemed to take no interest in the Christmas tree or the presents. Apparently, they had come only for dinner.

Watching the boys, I felt a wave of gratitude. How simple life is when you are a boy with loving parents, I thought. All you have to do is respect them, do what is expected, eat what you are given, and dream about all the things you would like to do in life, free of fear or concern for the future. These orphans probably had no idea who their parents were or even if they still lived. Did they wonder if their parents ever loved them? Did anybody treat them well? My heart went out to them. I struggled to control the urge to tell them that they had presents too. Perhaps they had so many disappointments in their short lives that this night did not mean all that much to them. Regardless of the indifference they probably felt from others, I imagined these two connected with each other through a powerful sense of loyalty and shared experience.

Mama called us to the dining room, where a succulent roasted turkey sat atop the table. Steam rose from it and filled the house with a wonderful aroma. We also had potatoes, vegetables, panetón (a kind of fruitcake traditionally served at Christmas), and hot chocolate. We all sat while Papa prayed and thanked God for what we had and for our special guests. Mama served each of us, and we started to eat.

As we enjoyed the meal, the boys spoke only when Mama gently tried to include them in the conversation. I didn't know what to say to our guests. Mama asked them if they wanted more. They politely nodded, but their expressions remained fixed and noncommittal. Unprompted, they never said a word throughout the meal. I had no idea what they might have had on their minds. Were they already thinking of ways to excuse themselves after eating so they could return to the orphanage? Logic indicated they had no real reason to get too excited about what was going on here tonight. My own feelings swirled. I looked forward to seeing their reactions when they opened their presents, but I also felt sad that they would be going back to life in the orphanage without a family to love them.

After dinner, we headed into the living room to pray before the nativity scene in accordance with the best Peruvian Catholic tradition. Ernesto and Gloria, the two youngest, put the figure of the baby Jesus between Mary and Joseph. We heard fireworks going off all over town. Then we all hugged each other and said, *"Feliz Navidad! Feliz Navidad!"*

The short but solemn ceremony concluded, and we moved excitedly to the Christmas tree to open presents. My brother Enrique and I sat on a sofa opposite our guests. The rest of the family sat in a nearly full circle facing the Christmas tree. All of the presents had names attached, except for the ones Enrique and I wrapped just before dinner.

The youngest children opened their presents first. Then we took turns going around the circle, ending with Mama and

Papa. Every so often I glanced over at our guests. They sat impassively as before, not sharing in the festive spirit of Christmas as they watched us opening presents.

Finally, only two presents remained, the largest ones. Our guests looked on politely, still unaware that anything special awaited them. I watched them closely for some kind of reaction, but they remained guarded and detached. I thought they might suspect something when all the presents had been claimed except for two. If they did, they didn't show it.

Enrique looked at me as if to say, "Okay, now what?" Clearly, he had also been watching our guests.

Pointing to the last two presents under the tree, Mama smiled at the two orphan boys and announced, "Those presents are for you."

Their jaws dropped, and their eyes opened wide as they stared at Mama. Then they shut their mouths and looked at each other as if they didn't know what to do next. Maybe they thought it might be some kind of cruel joke. If they did, they didn't think that for long. They stood up and moved quickly to the tree. You could see curiosity, excitement, and hope animating their faces.

They tore off the wrapping paper, unfolded their jackets and held them at arm's length, and gazed upon their gifts with wonder. They quickly put on their jackets, racing to see who could get his on first. The taller one got Enrique's jacket, and the shorter one got mine. It was plain to see right away that my jacket was a little too big for the shorter one, and Enrique's was too small for the taller one.

For a brief moment, we looked on uncomfortably, not knowing what to say or do. Our guests frowned momentarily, but then their faces brightened again. Not for nothing had they grown up struggling to survive! They knew how to solve problems and make decisions quickly. They looked at each other, and, without a word, they exchanged jackets. This time, the jackets fit perfectly.

We all clapped our hands and cheered. They looked at us and smiled for the first time. They looked truly happy, appreciative—and a little shy. They thanked and hugged Mama first, then Papa. Then they went around hugging the rest of us. They were still wearing their jackets when they left.

• Chapter Five •

A CLOSED DOOR

As I endured the daily grind of high school, the career I imagined fighting terrorism seemed a long way off. That all changed once I graduated. Suddenly, it was time to get really serious. Whatever ideals or aspirations I might have had meant nothing if I didn't get into officer school.

At that time, about 3,000 young men applied to Officer School of the Army every year, but only 150 were accepted for admission. I understood the brutal nature of the competition. Add to that some desperate times—with a struggling economy, high unemployment, and remote prospects for better conditions. On that day, good opportunities for a person just starting out in life were few and far between. Public institutions of higher education were in turmoil because of frequent strikes and demonstrations, and the high cost of tuition put education at a private institution out of reach for most. Despite the odds, I gave it my best shot.

Applicants were instructed to report to the officer school for medical examinations at a specified time and date. When we arrived, they divided us into groups of 300—with subgroups of twenty—based on the time we registered. Ranked military personnel began testing us to determine our personal health status and suitability for military service. Tests included a general physical examination, visual acuity test, audiology examination, x-rays, electrocardiogram, lab tests, an inventory of identifying marks on our bodies, and so on.

A few days later, we returned to learn the results of the medical tests and whether we would advance to the next step in the admissions process. Only 20 percent or so of candidates were disqualified. They told most of us to return the following week with gym clothes appropriate for the next round of tests.

As ordered, we arrived on examination day at 6:00 in the morning, even though the tests wouldn't begin until 8:00. We dressed in our gym clothes and headed to the athletic field where the testing would take place. Once we assembled in the original groups of twenty, we proceeded to designated areas of the field and waited to be told what to do next.

Each candidate would be scored according to how well he did in the 100-meter dash, 1.6-meter (one mile) run, the long jump, pull-ups, and swimming.

We began with pull-ups—with a minimum of twelve pull-ups required to pass. To receive the maximum score of 100 points, a candidate had to do eighteen pull-ups. At the end of the testing process, only the candidates with the highest cumulative scores would be accepted into the Officer School of the Army. So, it wasn't just good enough to pass, we had to score high on every section to be included among the best.

To get into position for the pull-ups, the candidate climbed a ten-foot pole to a horizontal bar. Then, grabbing the bar with hands and palms facing out, the candidate would hang with his arms straight and legs dangling. Finally, he would pull himself up until his chin was over the bar before lowering himself down again. Each candidate repeated this procedure until he wasn't able to pull himself up again or until he did eighteen pull-ups.

I had not anticipated this. When I practiced pull-ups at home, I did twenty or twenty-one pull-ups using a bar I could jump up to. I didn't have to climb a pole. Also, I practiced with my palms facing in, not out. Would that make a difference? I didn't know. Suddenly, I didn't feel so confident.

When my turn came, I forced myself to relax. I climbed up the pins on one of the two wooden poles that held the bar. As I hung there, it felt like my body weighed more by being suspended in the air ten feet off the ground. I told myself that it was just my imagination. I felt sure all the other candidates thought the same thing.

As I did the first pull-up, I realized that having my palms face out meant that my arm and chest muscles worked differently. As I pulled myself up, my upper body came away from the bar more, making other parts of my arms work harder. I did the first ten pull-ups without difficulty. Then I began to feel pain. I did twelve, thirteen, fourteen. But with the sun hot on my face, I debated stopping when I reached fifteen. But when I got to fifteen, I felt like I could manage one more. I kept telling myself, "One more, one more, one more," until I got to eighteen. I did it! One hundred points on pull-ups!

The captain recording our scores looked surprised as if to say, "Where did this skinny kid come from?" I walked away feeling good, even though my upper arms hurt and trembled with fatigue. I thought, One test down, four to go!

I assumed I'd be able to relax between each round of testing, but that wasn't the case. Waiting in line, watching fellow candidates tensed my body and put my mind on edge.

The next nerve-racking test? The long jump. To get 100 points, the jump had to be at least six meters. The idea was to run as fast as you could up to a white line and jump as far as possible. The captain would measure the distance from the white line up to where a part of your body touched the sand. This could be the back of your feet or your butt. If you stepped on the white line or jumped a few centimeters past it, they deducted points from your score. Your timing had to be just right when making the jump.

Before this, my best jumps had been between 5.50 and 5.75 meters. When it was my turn, I left my bag and walked to the spot where I would begin my run. The captain counted, "One, two, three." He blew his whistle. I ran to beat the devil, knowing I had one shot. Bringing my foot down about a centimeter in front of the white line, I launched myself forward, my arms and legs pumping. I bent my body forward as my feet came down to avoid landing on my butt and shortening my jump. My jump measured 5.85 meters—my longest ever—and one of the best in my group. Okay, two tests down, and three to go!

I felt good, but I still couldn't relax. Most of the candidates I competed against had two or three years on me. Still, I had completed two of the tests with good scores. That lifted my confidence, but only a little.

As we moved to the opposite side of the field for the 100-meter dash, the pain in my arms grew worse. The pain and anxiety would not go away.

To earn 100 points in the 100-meter dash, the candidate had to run the distance in twelve seconds or less. At the preparatory institute, we had been instructed to run as hard as we could while staring straight ahead, pumping our arms rhythmically along with our legs. I was a good long-distance runner, but speed was not my strength. Still, I thought I would do well enough.

I kept telling myself to be calm. After all, the other candidates only had two legs and two arms, just like I did. I thought they were probably as anxious and unsure of themselves as I was. I imagined some of them felt desperate, especially if they hadn't done well on previous tests.

Ten of us raced at a time. Once we got into the starting position, the captain called, "Ready, set, go!" The whistle blew, and we were off. We ran like starving wolves chasing a rabbit. We were no longer colleagues; we were competitors. We all knew that a poor performance could mean elimination.

I focused on the goal line. At the halfway mark, I was third or fourth—not too bad—then I realized that other runners were catching up and were nearly even with me. My legs burned, and I was breathing hard and fast, but I still had some energy in reserve. I gave it all I had. I passed one more runner and finished second. I did not complete the race in twelve seconds or less, but I knew my time was among the best. Three down, two to go!

I was doing well, and that comforted me, but my arms still hurt, and now so did my legs. Also, I was hungry. I had eaten only a light breakfast around 5:00, afraid that too much food might hurt my performance. We weren't allowed to bring snacks or food on the field during the tests. I could see that others in my group were also tired and hungry. We had been exerting ourselves under a blazing sun, and by midmorning, we were all hot, tired, and hungry.

After each test, we waited for the group ahead of us to finish before moving on. Around 10:00, we were told to line up for the 1.6-kilometer run.

"Ready, set, go!" The whistle blew, and twenty young men took off running. We had trained for this moment and knew how important it was. We all felt intense pressure. After the first lap of four around the track, I accelerated and passed a few runners, moving steadily toward the front of the pack.

I concentrated on the track ahead of me, focusing on what I had to do: Inhale deeply through your nose, exhale through your mouth. I kept telling myself, "Do your best!"

After the second lap, I forced myself to increase my pace, and I passed still more runners. I breathed deeply, inhaling and exhaling rhythmically. My strides were long and purposeful. I passed enough runners to move into third place.

At the 400-meter mark, I went all out. I moved into second place, determined to take the lead, but the lead runner kept blocking my way, preventing me from moving around him.

I stayed with him, only one step behind for another 250 meters. With 150 meters to go, I made my move, pulling even with him before he could block me again.

We sprinted side by side, listening to each other breathe, matching each other step for step. Looking straight ahead, I reached deep inside myself, calling up my last reserves of strength. With a final burst of speed, I took the lead with just sixty meters to go. The air streamed past my face as I ran. I could feel the sun on my face. My legs burned. I wasn't getting enough air, but I didn't care. Thirty meters, 10, 5. I crossed the finish line. I won! I think my time was around 4 minutes, 45 seconds. I earned one hundred points—again—and felt really good. Four events down. Only the swimming test remained.

We returned to the gym to change into our trunks. My triceps burned, and I was more tired and hungrier than before. As we walked into the pool area, we were surprised to learn that the swimming test was divided into three parts—racing 25 meters, jumping from the high diving board, and floating for three minutes. We knew that everyone before us had gone through the same tests, so we resigned ourselves to pushing through. We were told to remain silent unless asked a direct question, so we did not speak while we waited.

Around noon, my group was called. The sun was directly above us. Getting into the pool felt refreshing, but I didn't relax. I had only learned to swim a few weeks earlier, so I wasn't especially confident about how well I would do. I told myself, "This is just another test. You can do this. Just do the best you can."

I recalled the advice my cousin Miguel, a medical student, had given me when I told him how worried I was about the swimming part of the test. "When you jump, push out as hard and far as you can with your legs. Keep your body straight as a board and your hands out in front, and don't let your head and upper body go under as you hit the water. Your body will slide forward. Then swim for your life!"

I thought about his advice as I got into position with my knees bent, waiting for the signal to jump. "Ready, set, go." The whistle blew. I sprung out as far as I could and came down hard, feeling a slap of pain on my chest as I smacked the water. Immediately, I got into the rhythm of moving my arms and legs in coordination. I heard swimmers on either side of me, but I tried to block them out. Instead, I concentrated on staying in my lane and moving forward.

I had no idea how far ahead or behind I was. I only thought about reaching the finish line. Once again, I gave it everything I had. I finished second! I could hardly believe it! Not too shabby for someone who had learned to swim only a few weeks before. I couldn't relax too much, though. The swimming examination wasn't over yet. The jump from the high board and the floating part of the test were still to come.

Most of the others in my group looked scared as they climbed to the top of the platform and walked out onto the high board. It struck me as comical, almost absurd. How in the world did these men expect to get into the army if they were afraid to be eighteen or twenty feet up over the water?

Some of them froze in place on the board, terrified looks on their faces. When that happened, the captain, standing on a steady platform next to the diving board, just pushed them off.

At the foot of the ladder, the diving board didn't seem that high. After all, we were jumping into water, not rocks. I had never before jumped from such a height, but I thought it would be okay. As I climbed the ladder, I determined I would not look down. I would only stare straight ahead.

We were instructed to stand at the end of the diving board and cover our noses with one hand and our testicles with the other. When we jumped, we were to cross our legs. All of this raced through my mind when my name was called, signaling me to move forward onto the board.

Suddenly I realized what had unnerved the candidates ahead of me. The diving board was wet and slippery. The springy board bounced with every step I took, making me feel like I was about to fall off. My legs felt like jelly as I inched unsteadily to the end of the board. When I stopped, the board continued to bounce up and down, and I stood there feeling shaky.

Then, I looked down. Big mistake! The water churned below as if it had a life of its own. My heart beat in my chest until I thought it would explode. I could hear the blood pounding in my ears. I don't know how I did it, but I jumped, trembling inside as I stepped off the board.

My body plunged into the pool's depth. I finally stopped sinking and propelled myself toward the surface, desperately short of breath. I broke the surface gasping for air. But I'd done it! Finally, all the difficult parts of the swimming test were over—or so I thought. All that was left was to float for three minutes.

I learned to float in the Pacific Ocean, but the pool water was different from salt water. Salt water is more buoyant than fresh water, and I couldn't get the hang of floating in what felt like dense water. As hard as I tried to float, I felt myself sinking and began to panic. Forcing down my fear, I started dog paddling. I made myself hold my body erect in the water, rhythmically moving my feet and hands slowly back and forth. We had to float for only three minutes, but it was the longest three minutes of the entire day.

The tests were finally over—and not a moment too soon. After I swam to the edge of the pool, I nearly collapsed. I simply could not lift myself out. My triceps wouldn't work. I had to use my legs to push myself up and out of the pool.

I was so tired I fell asleep on the bus on the way home. Mama had aji de gallina waiting for me. Aji de gallina is delicious, shredded chicken prepared curry-style in a thick sauce made with milk, cream, ground walnuts, cheese, and aji amarillo (Peruvian yellow chili peppers), which gives it a rich, stew-like consistency. This mild but flavorful sauce, with just a hint of *aji*, is tempered by the cream and cheese. The shredded chicken and creamy spicy sauce are often served on a bed of rice with boiled potatoes and half a boiled egg on the side. I ate a couple platefuls of the delicious stew, then went straight to bed.

Three days later, we returned to the army base to learn the results of the examinations. An officer called out the names of the candidates who had passed. I felt elated when I heard my name. All the hard work over the past several months had paid off.

Those who had passed the physical fitness tests were ordered to return the next day at 6:00 a.m. This time, we were not separated into smaller groups. We were to be subjected to a battery of standardized psychometric tests over a seven-hour period. The tests assessed mathematical reasoning, reading comprehension, problem-solving, language skills, vocational aptitude, logic, and so on. We also took a personality inventory test.

We had time to loosen up and talk to each other a bit before things got started that day. Doing so helped calm our nerves. Several of the candidates were students from prestigious universities like San Marcos and Universidad Nacional de Ingenieria (UNI).

I had to ask, "How come you guys are trying to get into the army when you are already in such distinguished universities?"

They all said pretty much the same thing. They had experienced too many strikes, too many disruptions. Classes would be canceled with no grades issued. They lost credits for classes they'd worked hard to complete. They were tired of the constant Communist propaganda on campus and frustrated when professors didn't show up for lectures because they were afraid of being killed. At the rate things were going, it might be ten or more years before they graduated, they said. They had registered for Officer School of the Army because they no longer felt like they could pursue their hopes and dreams.

The seven hours of testing became a grueling ordeal of mental prowess. When it was over, I felt like we had been tested more for our stamina and endurance to see how well we would hold up with no rest and no food. Again, we were ordered to return the following week to learn the test results.

When we went back, tensions were high. We realized the mental exams might eliminate many of us, so we were sensitive to each other's feelings as we waited for the announcement of the test results. I was thrilled when I heard my name called, and I did my best to console those who didn't make the cut. Fewer than half of us advanced to the next level of testing.

The next round tested our academic skills and general knowledge. Once again, we arrived before sunrise to wait for the testing to begin at 8:00. The first three hours focused on Peruvian and world history, writing skills, reading comprehension, and Spanish literature. The next three hours focused on mathematics and the natural sciences.

After hours and hours of reading, writing, analyzing, and

struggling to recall mathematical formulas without the aid of a calculator, my brain felt ready to shut down in protest. I'm sure the others in my group felt the same way. I struggled mightily with calculus and didn't finish that section.

Those from San Marcos and UNI appeared to have an easier time finishing the science and math sections. I tried not to think too much about it, telling myself to put it behind me and stay focused on the next challenge.

The following week, we all felt the strain when we returned to learn the results of the academic tests. Only five hundred of us would be selected to move on to the next level. I felt immense relief to hear my name called off once again.

The last part of the examination process was the personal interview and cultural awareness test. Only 150 of the remaining 500 candidates would be accepted for Officer School of the Army, based on the results of the personal interview. Seven of every ten of the remaining candidates were about to be eliminated. I cannot stress enough how important this part of the process was.

The candidates had heard rumors about how the personal interviews would be structured. One scenario had each candidate presented with a number of plates, cups, silverware, and other dining room accouterments on a table. The candidate would then be asked to identify the purpose of each item and to arrange it properly in relation to the other items.

Most of us came from humble backgrounds with little or no exposure to the finer nuances of etiquette, so the idea of this made us feel uncomfortable.

Another possibility was more provocative. We imagined ourselves entering a room with the interviewing team of officers. A beautiful woman in a bikini would be sitting in a corner. The interviewers would closely watch the candidate for his reaction. If the finalist spent too much time gawking at the young woman, he might be judged to be a possible sexual deviant. On the other hand, if the candidate did not look at all, that might indicate something else. I remember hearing some pretty wild speculations about how this might go.

Other rumors circulated, as well, but in the final analysis, the most reliable indication of what to expect came from the preparatory institute. The institute classes emphasized general knowledge in areas such as the population demographics of Peru, current events and governmental affairs, and awareness of other countries.

We were expected to wear a clean, pressed suit, tie, dress shirt, and shiny, well-polished shoes to the personal interview. By now, most of us who were left knew each other, and we all wished one another well. We lined up in single file along one side of a hallway. One by one, we entered the room where we would be interviewed by the general and his committee of officers. Each interview lasted only a few minutes. Afterward, the candidate exited by a different door, so as not to have any contact with waiting candidates.

When my turn came, I entered the room and tried to project a confidence I didn't feel. There was no beautiful woman in a bikini sitting in a corner. Oh, good. There was no table with dishes and silverware, either.

The director of the officer school, a general, sat in the middle of a long table with officers on either side of him. As I crossed the floor and stood in front of them, none of them looked up at me. This action alone felt very intimidating. A lieutenant ordered—not asked—me to take a seat. I sat and looked at the imposing group of men, trying to quell the butterflies in my stomach.

The lieutenant told me that I had done well overall, including the section covering general knowledge, but I had not done as well in math. He directed me to solve the equation on the blackboard to my right.

I looked at the equation and froze. The calculus problem

mocked me, and I had no idea how to solve it. I just sat, staring at the board, not moving or saying anything. After what might have been a long minute or so, I was told that I could leave. I had been dismissed.

I left the room feeling wretched, discouraged, and defeated.

Papa was home waiting for me that afternoon. He usually didn't get home until after 7:00 in the evening.

"How did it go?" he asked carefully, seeing how stressed I looked. I gave it to him straight, with no embellishments.

"Damn!" Papa spat out angrily. "They did that because they were looking for ways to eliminate people."

Papa believed in me, and I was afraid that I let him down. Still, I wanted to think there might be some reason for hope, however unlikely that might be.

I went back to the military base in late February with great trepidation to hear the final roll call of candidates who had been accepted to Officer School of the Army. The sun blazed hot that morning. The general and several officers were present. All of us wore suits. A captain began calling the names of the new cadets of the Military School of Peru. One hundred and fifty new cadets would soon have their aspirations realized. The other 350 candidates would go home brokenhearted.

As more and more new cadets stepped forward to be congratulated, my spirits sank. Finally, the captain stopped the roll call. My name had not been called. For several long minutes I stood there disconsolate, my gut clenched tight.

For a while, I just wanted to be left alone with my thoughts and my bitter disappointment. Fortunately, I didn't brood long. If I had learned anything in life, it was that feeling sorry for myself didn't make things better. Self-pity was a waste of time. I needed to take actions and start getting ready for next year's competition, practice more math, especially calculus.

I decided not to let it bother me anymore. After all, almost no one was ever accepted into Officer School of the Army on the first try. My brother Edgar tried three times before he was accepted into Officer School of the National Guard. I turned my thoughts to preparing for next year's competition. I resumed my training schedule and that helped.

That summer, I began working as a construction helper at the company where Papa worked part time. My duties included mixing sand, cement, and water for concrete and mortar. I also helped lay out building foundations. I made the framework to hold the concrete in place until it dried. I thought I got rather good at what I did. I also helped pour asphalt, lifting and pushing a deep wheelbarrow full of tarmac for surfacing roads.

I took pride in my work. It was fascinating to see streets, recreational areas, and buildings emerge from the raw materials we used. I reveled in the results of our labors.

I worked during the day and studied at night. When I retook the entrance examinations for officer school the next year, I was determined to do even better than last year. I especially studied calculus.

The work I did with the construction company helped to build up my strength and endurance. I filled out more, and my muscle mass increased, especially in my arms and legs. I also ran each morning before going to work. I was determined not to fail next time.

• Chapter Six •

THE DETECTIVE ACADEMY

In early May 1983, on behalf of the construction company I worked for, I participated in a door-to-door survey of residents living around a major park in San Isidro, a suburb of Lima. The company was gathering data concerning the need for additional recreational facilities, such as tennis courts and micro soccer fields. The company sent the survey results to the mayor of the district, who then presented them to the City Council for consideration of funding.

After about a week with the survey team, I was riding a minibus to a neighborhood to conduct the survey, when I saw a large group of young men standing in front of the Escuela de Oficiales de la Policía de Investigaciones del Perú, or more simply, the detective academy. The detective academy is different from the Officer School for the Army. A number of the young men looked familiar. I thought I recognized some of them from the officer school entrance examinations.

I got off the minibus to find out what was going on. The detective academy was a silver and light gray, six-story building that took up the entire block. It had recently launched a new accelerated recruitment program. The admissions process would begin in late May, and the new cadets would start classes the first week in July.

I bought the admissions handbook and began reading it on the minibus as I commuted to and from work. I learned Peru had an acute shortage of detectives and policemen. To some degree, the shortage was due to the increased violence being perpetrated by terrorists. Cities needed more detectives and policemen to wage the war on terrorism. Terrorist organizations had been particularly effective at targeting the military and police for assassination, creating a shortage and crisis in leadership. Because of the threat to national security, cadet training at the detective academy was abbreviated so graduates could go into active service as quickly as possible. Instead of four years, the cadets who started in July would finish in three and a half years.

I finished going through the handbook later that night. I found the program description very appealing. This entity was responsible for fighting organized crime and was in charge of divisions such as the antidrug-dealers, antiterrorism, kidnapping, money laundering, homicide, and secret service. The admissions process for the detective academy was not so different from the one at the Officer School of the Army. It sounded like the kind of program I wanted to be part of.

When Papa got home that night, we talked about my interest in the detective academy. I told him I wanted to register for the program, but I wouldn't do it without his support. In essence, I was asking the family to make another financial commitment on my behalf.

Papa didn't say much as I explained why I thought it was

a good idea. For the most part, he trusted my judgment. When he asked questions, he did so to make sure I'd considered everything.

"Well, hijo, this is unexpected," he said slowly. "I didn't think you would be needing help again this soon, but go ahead. We'll make it work."

I knew I was asking for a lot, but Papa actually looked pleased that I was taking the initiative now rather than waiting until next year.

The entrance examination process for the detective academy was as rigorous as the one for admission to the Officer School for the Army. This time, as I went to the various exams, I felt more confident and better prepared, and I passed all the tests with high scores. When it came down to the personal interview at the end, I had time to think about my situation.

I had done well so far, I knew, but that didn't necessarily mean much. I thought I had done well before and look where that got me. I was determined not to go into the personal interview over-confident. I pored over my notes on the various countries of the world, trying to commit them to memory— their capital cities, heads of state, demographics, currencies, and commerce. I memorized the Peruvian political divisions, names of secretaries and ministers, names of past presidents, and studied important current events.

The setting for the personal interview was eerily similar to the one at the officer school. Tensions among the final candidates ran high. This final test would determine our futures. Some of us had made it this far before, but that didn't make it any less stressful.

I had freshly cut short hair and wore a pressed suit, tie, white shirt, and black, polished shoes to the interview. I looked good and knew it. I refused to be disqualified because of the way I presented myself.

When I walked into the interview room, I stood before the

panel of interviewers. They sat at a long table, very much like the one at the officer school. The main difference was that they wore dark suits, not uniforms. The detectives mostly worked undercover. They usually wore plain clothes to avoid identification as law enforcement officers. Even so, their wearing suits instead of uniforms did not make the process any less intimidating.

The director of the detective academy, a general, sat in the middle, with officers on either side.

"Mr. Serván, you did very well on all your exams," one of the officers began. I tensed up. Those were almost the exact words the lieutenant had spoken to start my interview at the officer school before he presented me with a question I could not answer. I dreaded what would come next.

"Tell us the names of all the ministers of our country." His expression revealed nothing.

I relaxed. Civics was one of my favorite subjects. I paid close attention to current events, so I was not intimidated by his question.

I looked at the officer calmly for a moment to steady myself. Then I named all the thirteen national government ministers and the departments they headed. At the conclusion of my recitation, no one smiled. No one said anything. They all looked at me impassively. When they finally dismissed me, the general instructed me to return the following evening at 6:00 p.m. to hear the roll call of new cadets who would enter the detective academy in July.

I left the interview believing I had done well, but I still wondered if my overall scores had been good enough. The competition was tough. Only the most superior candidates would be selected.

Papa was waiting for me at home that evening after the interview. "How did it go, hijo?" Right to the point.

I recounted the events at the interview objectively, trying

not to sound too confident or boastful.

"So, tell me the names of the thirteen ministers," Papa ordered more than asked.

I think he wanted to see how quickly I would recite the list. Looking steadily back at Papa, I named the ministers easily. When I finished, I thought I saw a look of satisfaction cross his face.

The next day, in spite of the dreary, overcast weather, I was cheerful and eager to hear the evening roll call of successful candidates. As the day progressed, however, I started second-guessing myself and feeling insecure.

A couple of hours before it was time to leave for the detective academy, Papa asked me if I wanted Mama and him to go along. He had asked me the same question on the day the roll call of new cadets for officer school was announced. My answer was the same as it was then. I didn't want my parents there because of what had happened when my brother Edgar failed to get into officer school.

Actually, Edgar failed the admissions process three times—once for Officer School for the Army and twice for the Republican Guard. Each time, Mama and Papa went with him to hear the roll call of new cadets, and each time they were disappointed. My memory of the last time was especially vivid.

On the day the announcement was made, my parents and Edgar left for the Republican Guard headquarters early in the morning, full of optimism. The rest of us stayed home, waiting excitedly, expecting good news. When 2:00 p.m. came and they had not returned, we speculated that maybe they had stopped at a restaurant for lunch to celebrate before coming home.

I went outside every few minutes to look for Edgar and my parents. When I finally saw them, my heart sank. Edgar and Papa were on either side of Mama. They walked slowly, dragging their feet. They looked tired, dejected, and crestfallen. I had never seen a sadder sight. They looked sorrowful and distressed like someone had died. I ran back into the house. With a knot in my throat, I told my brothers and sisters what I had seen. Veronica cautioned all of us not to say anything and just to wait.

When they came in, we looked at them expectantly but said nothing. Papa asked if we had had lunch yet. Veronica said that we were waiting for them to come home, and Papa asked her to serve lunch because Mama needed to rest. Edgar looked thoroughly demoralized and embarrassed. Mama came out after a bit to help Veronica with lunch. We were all quiet and sad.

On his fourth attempt, Edgar was accepted for cadet training, but the three previous disappointments overshadowed the eventual victory. I thought my chances of being accepted were very good, but I didn't want to put my parents through that kind of disappointment again if I didn't make the roll call. Papa seemed to understand when I told him that I preferred to go by myself. I would rather be alone if the news were bad.

When it was finally time to go, I kissed Mama on the forehead, and she wished me good luck. I knew Mama would be praying for me. Papa gave me an earnest look and put his hand on my shoulder for support.

Riding on the minibus to the detective academy, I thought about how my life was about to turn in a profoundly different direction. I felt oddly conflicted with high anxiety and a strange kind of serenity.

We assembled outside of a walled-off area on the south side of the detective academy called the Court of Honor. When I arrived at twilight, hundreds of candidates, most with parents and other relatives and some with girlfriends, were already there waiting.

Shortly after 6:00 p.m., the large south door to the Court

of Honor opened. Only the candidates were allowed in. Everyone else waited outside. Dark clouds created a gray, somber setting for the proceedings. My breath was visible in the cold, wintry air. The other candidates and I, now colleagues and no longer competitors, stood chatting pleasantly, wishing each other well.

A captain stepped to the podium on a raised platform in the front of the Court of Honor. When he began speaking, we all stopped talking and came sharply to attention. He told us that 250 candidates had been selected for cadet training at the detective academy and that their names would be called according to their ratings or scores. Upon hearing his name, each candidate was to raise his right hand, speak out to indicate his presence, and run to the right side of the Court of Honor. After concluding the roll call of new cadets, everyone not called would have to leave the area immediately.

The captain opened a folder and began the roll call. I hung on every name, my anxiety and anticipation increasing every time I was not called. My heart beat fast with anticipation and excitement, but also dread.

When a name was called, each candidate threw up his right hand and yelled, *"presente!"* and ran to the side of the Court of Honor to stand in formation at attention, eyes straight ahead. A couple of lieutenants made sure the new cadets stood still and did not speak to each other.

A few long minutes passed and my tension mounted. I was wound tight as a drum. Then I heard my full name called, "Serván Triveño, Carlos Rigoberto."

"Presente!" I shouted, nearly throwing my shoulder out of joint as my right hand shot up. I ran to join the other new cadets. I had made it! It was one of the most thrilling moments of my life! I don't believe I had ever cried from happiness before. At that moment I could have, but I didn't dare. The two lieutenants were scrutinizing us carefully, making sure that

we maintained the proper respect and demeanor. I stood there at attention and did not smile or move. We were expected to be mindful of the responsibility that we, as new cadets, were about to assume as members of a military institution. The highly momentous occasion dripped with rich tradition and meaning.

The roll call continued, but I heard nothing. Lost in emotion, I hardly even noticed the cold weather.

After the names of all 250 new cadets had been called, the unsuccessful candidates were asked to leave. Unfortunately, this didn't give us the chance to console some of them. When the officers and new cadets were alone in the Court of Honor, the colonel, chief of the School of Officers, moved forward to stand in front of us. Looking stern, he congratulated us and then got right down to business.

"You are now first-year cadets of the School of Officers for the Peruvian Investigation Police," the colonel shouted. "You are bound to all of our rules. You are expected to behave as gentlemen at all times, everywhere and anywhere you go. The day after tomorrow, on Saturday, there will be an inauguration ceremony for your class. You will be here tomorrow all day for rehearsal. Each of you will be given a list of items to bring with you. Be warned that if you do not bring all the items listed, you will learn how cadets are disciplined at this institution. On Saturday, you are to come with your head shaved. Make sure you wear a suit. You will not drink excessively, get into any kind of trouble, or stay out late. As of this moment, you are cadets. If we discover that you have not respected this code of honor, you will be expelled even before you check in. Congratulations once again. We will see you here tomorrow at 7:00 a.m. sharp."

The formalities concluded, we trotted in perfect formation through the building, exiting through the west door of the complex. Many parents and relatives waited for their loved ones—now cadets. Our excitement could not be contained. We fell over ourselves congratulating each other, smiling ear to ear. Everyone laughed and hugged. Some people cried. New cadets could be heard yelling, "I made it! I made it!"

In the thrill of the moment, I regretted not having my parents there. I even looked around for them, thinking that they might show up to surprise me. Of course, they weren't there. They respected me too much to go against my wishes.

I was tempted to grab and hug anyone close by, so strong was my emotion and excitement. However, I managed to control myself and walked swiftly to catch the bus to San Juan. On the way home, I looked for someone I knew from my neighborhood, work, or school—anyone. I wanted to share my good news with the world. The bus could not go fast enough.

I got off the bus at 9:00 p.m. and ran the ten blocks home. I would have stopped to share my great joy if I had seen any friends or neighbors outside, but no one was out that late. When I turned the corner to my neighborhood, I saw Papa's silhouette on the sidewalk outside our house. He stood looking in my direction. At first, I thought he looked tense or worried, but when he saw me running toward him, he relaxed. As I got closer, my exuberance was unmistakable. Then Papa smiled. Papa did not smile often. It was a rare occasion indeed! He actually beamed.

"So," he said, pride evident in his voice, "What's up, hijo?"

"I'm in! I'm in! I made it." My smile reached ear to ear, and I slowed down to a walk.

Papa gave me a big hug, again something that didn't happen often. He called to Mama, "Come out and look at your son, the second cadet in the family!" He beamed at me once more.

Mama hurried outside. Crying, she hugged me tightly. I kissed her on the forehead. I will never forget the faces of Mama and Papa glowing with love and pride as I hugged them.

We held onto each other, smiling, as we walked into the house. Mama couldn't stop crying. Was she happy because this was what I had been working so hard to achieve? Was she sad I wouldn't be living at home once I started cadet training? Was she afraid of the danger I might face because of the terrorists? Maybe she cried for all these reasons.

My brothers and sisters came out and hugged me as well, including Gloria and Ernesto. Gloria and Ernesto were only two and four years old and were not old enough to know what was going on, but they knew everyone was happy and having a good time. That was good enough for them.

Mama had a late dinner waiting for me, one of my favorites—lomo saltado, a mix of Chinese stir-fry and classic Peruvian cuisine. Tender strips of beef (occasionally you will find it made with alpaca meat) mixed with onions, tomatoes, aji chiles, and other spices. The ingredients are stir-fried together until the beef is cooked and the tomatoes and onions start to take on a gravy-like consistency. Lomo saltado is a very flavorful dish accompanied by french fries (potatoes are a staple in Peru) and a mound of steaming white rice.

To mark the significance of the occasion, Papa repeated something he often said. It had particular relevance today. "It is not the circumstances of birth that make a man; it is what he makes of himself. You will have ups and downs, but your strength of character will show as you get up after every fall. Always keep that in mind, hijo."

The next evening, friends and neighbors stopped by to celebrate my acceptance into the detective academy. Remarkably, Papa offered me my first glass of beer. We clinked glasses and drank to my future success. "*Salud!*" ("To your health!")

On the day of the inauguration ceremony, I felt a mix of anticipation and anxiety. I was eager to begin cadet training and take on new challenges, but I was also apprehensive about what was to come. The familiar, comfortable life I knew growing up would be left behind as I stepped forward to embrace a future fraught with uncertainties and danger. My spirit was buoyed, however, with the knowledge that this part of my journey would be shared with a group of young men intent on making a difference in the world. Once we completed our rigorous training, we would all be detectives!

Two hundred and fifty new cadets and their families arrived at the detective academy on that cloudy, cold, and misty morning in July, typical for Lima in winter. I was to be part of this group of cadets for the next three-and-a-half years. Before the start of the actual ceremony, ranking officers allowed us time for picture-taking with our parents and relatives to commemorate the day.

A captain gave the sign for us to assemble in formation, and our families went to the section reserved for them in the Court of Honor. The general thanked our parents for being present and welcomed the new cadets to a life of sacrifice, honor, and service to our country. The order was given for us to march forward in step with the trumpets and drums playing patriotic music on our left. The applause from the audience on our right grew as we approached the front. The music thundered as we reached the place where we were to stand. I reveled in the thrilling atmosphere. I had goosebumps. My heart beat furiously. Standing at parade rest, I looked straight ahead and listened to the applause and shouts from the families as the music around me built to a crescendo. I made a solemn oath to myself to work hard as a cadet and to do my best as a police officer.

At the conclusion of the inauguration ceremony, the band played as we marched from the Court of Honor and we made our way to the dormitory that would be our home. I was eager to begin the training that would prepare me for an exciting, rewarding career. Little did I know, hell was waiting for us!

• Chapter Seven •

BAPTISM BY FIRE

After the inauguration ceremony, we headed up the stairs near the east entrance of the detective academy to our dormitory rooms on the fifth floor. The fourth-year cadets waited for us on the second floor. As we came up the stairs, they began yelling, "Dogs, get down on your heels! Now!"

Stunned, I hesitated, not sure what to do. Some of the new cadets who were former soldiers or noncommissioned officers squatted as ordered, as if they knew what to expect. Seeing their immediate compliance, the rest of us quickly followed suit. We were ordered to remain crouching as we carried our luggage up the stairs. Most of us put our bags on our shoulders, finding it to be the easiest way to manage the load. The fourth-year cadets pushed down on our bags as we passed by to make our trek as difficult as possible. All the way up to our rooms on the fifth floor, they hurled insults at us and called us mangy, miserable dogs and good-for-nothing curs.

The 250 new cadets in my class were subdivided into five sections of 50 each. A fourth-year cadet was placed in charge as prefect or monitor of each section. The members of each section had the same schedule of classes and activities as others in that section.

I was assigned a bunk in one of the ten dormitory rooms designated for the new first-year cadets on the fifth floor of the detective academy. There were twelve or so two-man bunks, more or less, in each dormitory room lined up against opposite walls with an aisle running up the middle of the room. My room had fourteen bunks for twenty-eight cadets. Cadets sharing a dormitory room did not belong to any particular section. We were all first-year cadets, but we might not necessarily share the same schedule.

"You will be tested to see if you can adjust to life here. If you cannot, you are free to leave," the prefect in charge of my section said as if he couldn't care less.

As it turned out, eight cadets who couldn't adjust to military life opted out in the first couple of weeks. After a brief tour of our quarters, we were ordered to leave our bags and report to the Court of Honor to pick up our uniforms and receive further instructions.

Back in the Court of Honor, a captain threw bags to individual cadets when called. The bags contained our uniforms and other gear. One included our khaki, classroom, and dress uniforms. Other bags held our shirts, pants, sweatshirt, sweatpants, boots, and shoes. Still other bags contained our bedding and nightclothes—pillows, blankets, bed sheets, pajamas, towels, and robes. When a cadet didn't catch a bag, all of us had to squat and jump 300 times with our arms extended straight out in front of us, do fifty push-ups, and fifty jumping jacks.

As they say in the academy, "Punish all for the acts of one!"

We were instructed to sew our initials into our uniforms, make our beds, and organize our wardrobes. We were ordered to finish by noon and to dress in our khaki uniforms for lunch. The fourth-year cadets overseeing us that weekend ate lunch with us. The rest of the cadets at the academy were off duty until the evening of the next day, Sunday. We spent most of that Saturday and Sunday marking our belongings and exercising rigorously.

That weekend, the lieutenants constantly barked orders, giving us just thirty seconds to assemble in the Court of Honor and to get into formation. The last five cadets to arrive from each section were identified and disciplined at a later time. No one wanted extra punishment, of course, so we jumped like jackrabbits whenever the order to assemble came, but no matter how fast we moved, there were always five who were last.

Every time we assembled and stood at attention in the Court of Honor, the lieutenants would bark, "Arms to your sides! Suck in that gut! Tighten your butt! Chest out! Heads up! Look at the fifth floor! Don't move!" They shouted as loudly as possible, their orders interspersed with vulgar language and insults. Typically, we would be ordered to perform calisthenics, usually 200 jump squats and fifty push-ups.

"Are you tired?" the lieutenant would ask.

"No, sir!" we would shout in unison.

The lieutenant would shout back, "In that case, for your great pleasure, 100 more jump squats!"

Generally, this was followed by fifty more jumping jacks and twenty more push-ups. We were pushed to the limits of our physical endurance, which left us trembling with fatigue.

A lieutenant, seeing how shaky we were, yelled, "Are your legs and arms burning?"

If we answered, "Yes, sir!" the lieutenant would respond,

"Then blow on them to cool them off!" Not terribly sympathetic.

The strenuous exercises went on and on that Saturday and Sunday without a break. When we were finally allowed to return to our dormitories, we all ran to the common restroom facilities first to relieve ourselves. I heard someone cry out, "Oh man! I never thought urinating could give me more pleasure than sex!"

The captain stressed that we had to conduct ourselves as gentlemen at all times with all civilians, especially members of the opposite sex. After an hour or so of orientation to military life, we continued our exercises.

A lieutenant told us the rest of the cadets would return that Sunday evening from their weekend off, and we would learn more about life at the academy from the fourth-year cadets, who would serve as our mentors. That Sunday night, we collapsed into our beds, exhausted after a second long day of unrelenting exercise.

In the middle of the night, we woke from a deep sleep to the sound of shouting, "Everyone, attention!" The dormitory lights snapped on.

My fellow cadets and I jumped out of bed and snapped to attention. We stood in our green pajamas, bright light reflecting off our totally shaved heads. The person who had shouted walked through the room wearing a khaki uniform and carrying an automatic rifle.

"Mangy dogs are not supposed to sleep in beds!" he shouted. "Dogs like you sleep on the floor! Lie down on the floor, and sleep there!"

Twenty-eight cadets lay down on the hard floor as ordered, and the lights went out. Amazingly, we had no trouble falling back to sleep.

After what seemed like only a minute, another fourth-year cadet came in shouting, "All, attention!"

Once again, we jumped to our feet.

This fourth-year cadet wore a suit and carried a briefcase. Lowering his voice, he admonished, "You are now cadets with the investiture of a gentleman, and as such, you must conduct yourselves accordingly. It is denigrating to sleep on the floor. Gentlemen sleep in beds! When I finish counting to three, all of you are to be back in your beds. One, two, three!"

We were all back in our beds before he finished counting. The lights went out again, and he left.

After only a few minutes, another shout came. "All, attention!"

Yet again, we were up, standing at attention, tired and fuzzy-headed.

Another fourth-year cadet wearing a khaki uniform exclaimed, "Dogs don't sleep on beds! When I finish counting to three, you are to be lying between the mattress and the bed frame! One, two, three!"

Before he finished counting, we had all tucked ourselves between the mattresses and the bed frames. The mattress was made of foam rubber and was supported on thick metal springs. The mattress was seventy-four inches long, twenty-six inches wide, and three inches thick. Once again, we fell right back to sleep.

Lights on! Another shout! "All, attention! Mangy dogs, you dare to make a mess of the beds provided to you by the government from taxes paid by the people! Take off your pajamas and throw them in the aisle!"

After a few quick glances at each other, we did as we were told, wondering what would come next.

"I am going to count to ten," the fourth-year cadet said. "You will find and put on the right pajamas and get back into bed before I finish counting. If you take too long, all of you will stand at attention in the Court of Honor for the rest of the night."

The count started, and we scrambled like mad for our pajamas. Somehow, we all made it back to bed with our pajamas on—at least that is what we thought—before he finished counting.

The fourth-year cadet seemed satisfied. He told us to sleep well, turned the lights off, and left. I noticed that my pajamas were too short. We started whispering among ourselves, trying to identify the pajamas we had by the initials sewn into the fabric, using the faint light from a streetlight coming through the fifth-floor window.

The lights snapped back on! Another fourth-year cadet came charging in. "You are supposed to be sleeping, not talking in the middle of the night after curfew! Get in squat position! One, two!" he shouted.

Having learned the correct response, we answered back, "Three, four."

Once we were in position, the fourth-year cadet commanded us to do 200 jump squats. "Begin now!"

We did the 200 jump squats and counted out loud as we went. After that, we did thirty push-ups, 200 more jump squats, and twenty more push-ups. Finally, we were told to get some rest because hell was waiting for us the next day.

After a few minutes of trying to sleep, another fourth-year cadet came in and turned the lights back on. He was dressed in a uniform and carried an automatic rifle. He looked stony-faced with a grim expression, but his eyes glinted brightly, as if he were thoroughly enjoying the moment. For this reason, the dogs called him "Smiley Eyes."

"Have you guys prayed?" Smiley Eyes asked.

We looked at each other, mystified. What could be coming now? Someone nodded his head, and then the rest of us did the same.

"Tell me how you pray," Smiley Eyes asked, amusement still glinting in his eyes. He was enjoying himself.

Someone started to recite the Lord's Prayer hesitantly. "Our Father, Who art in Heaven ..."

"No, no," Smiley Eyes shouted. "That is not the prayer!"

Someone else began reciting the Hail Mary.

Smiley Eyes cut him off. "No, no! That is not right either!"

Baffled by his cryptic command, we looked at each other blankly.

Finally, Smiley Eyes enlightened us. "You need to pray the Almighty prayer! See, Godsons, as first-year cadets, you are dogs. The second-year cadets are old dogs, and their class is called the Valiants. Third-year cadets are godmothers, and their class is called the Intrepids. The fourth-year cadets are the godfathers, and our class is named the Almighty." He smiled openly now, having a grand old time with us.

"So, the prayer goes like this: 'Oh, you Almighty, you who control all the floors in this building, even the hallways, I submit my dog's soul and body to you. Almighty, free us from the punishment of the Valiants and the Intrepids. Almighty now and forever and ever, amen!'"

Smiley Eyes made us repeat the Prayer of the Almighty several times until we memorized it. Then, still smiling, he told us to go to bed with reassurances that our prayers would be heard and that we would be protected. After that, the lights went out again. However, we were not destined to get much rest that night.

Shortly thereafter, around 2:00 a.m., another godfather came in and shouted, "All, attention!" By this time, we were used to the outbursts and were up quickly, standing at attention. The fourth-year cadet wore a khaki uniform and a kind of ski mask called a *pasa montaña* (passing through the mountains), commonly worn by people in the Andes, where the temperature often falls below zero. We nicknamed him "The Masked One."

He strutted up and down the middle of the room, shouting

orders and hurling imprecations. "Not fast enough! Not fast enough! Terrorists move quickly, and you need to be fast!"

He ordered us back to bed and, after a short interval, again shouted, "All, attention!"

We scrambled back up and stood at attention as ordered, but we weren't fast enough for The Masked One. He ordered us back to bed and up again another ten times or so before he was satisfied and turned the lights out and left.

A few minutes later, another shout, "All, attention!" This time, the godfather sniffed the air and acted as if he smelled something truly offensive. "Stinky dogs. You did not wash and did not put talcum powder on your feet! It smells like llama jerky! Go to the bathroom and wash your stinky feet and use talcum powder! You have five minutes!"

We got our soap, sandals, and towels. It was winter, and the water was cold. We were tired and miserable, but we all knew that we were going through a rite of passage that would bind us closer together. We just had to tolerate it and support each other. I remember a fellow cadet offering this encouragement, "Don't worry, *promo*. This will last for only a few days. It will be over soon." *("Promoción"* refers to a class of students or cadets; *"promo"* is a term equivalent to "classmate.")

After we showered, we returned to our sleeping quarters, put talcum powder on our feet, and went back to bed. But not for long.

Another command came just a few minutes later. "All, attention!"

As we stood at attention, the godfather walked down the aisle inspecting the floor between the bunk beds. "Dirty dogs, someone left talcum powder all over the floor! Get your wax and start waxing!"

Resigned, we cleaned and waxed the floor as ordered. Afterward, we washed our hands and returned to bed with little real hope of uninterrupted sleep. The same godfathers came back several times with other creative torments. From time to time, we could hear similar disturbances going on in the other first-year dormitory rooms. At 4:00 in the morning, they finally left us alone to get what little sleep we could.

At 5:30, the morning alarm woke us with a start. We had two minutes to get into our exercise clothes, run down to the Court of Honor, and get into formation. As always, the last five cadets to assemble would be punished for their tardiness, so we ran as fast as we could. We took the stairs three at a time down the five floors of the detective academy to stand in formation in the Court of Honor.

Our godfathers told us we needed to inherit their self-discipline and excellent grades. They said every class or promoción at the detective academy was unique and had a name of its own, distinct from the names of all other classes. We were told to start thinking about what we wanted our class to be called.

We competed with other classes in sports, such as soccer, karate, boxing, and track and field. Everything we did was as a unit. We were not individual cadets competing against each other, we were part of a unified whole. There was a tremendous sense of group loyalty or *esprit de corps* that gave us pride in who we were.

Many of us became good friends with our bunkmates, calling each other *camacho* or *camachito*. "*Cama*" means "bed." We were assigned guard duty together and sat next to each other in class. When a cadet was missing, officers expected his *camacho* to know where he was.

Many of the cadets from the higher classes proved to be good role models, and we found it a privilege to work with and learn from them. We respected these conscientious mentors for what they taught us.

At all meals, the dogs served food to the godfathers, godmothers, and old dogs. Six cadets sat at each table. For breakfast, we made ham sandwiches and served them with oatmeal and coffee.

At noon, we ladled soup and offered the main dish, with the largest piece of meat going to the godfathers, before serving the rest of the table. We repeated the same procedure at dinnertime.

In the early days of cadet training, the godfathers would mix our soup, salad, main dish, and dessert together into an unappetizing mess that we had to eat without complaint. Sometimes it was enough to make us gag, but, of course, we knew that any protest or sign of displeasure would be immediately punished.

We were required to sit straight in our chairs and use our forks or spoons to lift our food to our mouths without bending our heads. If we spilled, we had to do more exercises and/or stand at attention in the Court of Honor for a couple of hours.

Most of the godfathers and officers were strict disciplinarians. For the most part, they limited punishment to additional exercise. Many of the godfathers and officers exercised with the cadets, showing they valued physical fitness, but a few of the upper-level cadets and officers seemed to enjoy their authority a little too much, deriving undue pleasure from the inventive orders they gave us. For instance, as we were about to do push-ups, they might pour water from the toilet onto the floor underneath us. If any part of our body or our khaki uniforms touched the dirty water, they would order us to do additional exercises or to stand at attention in the Court of Honor after lights out until around 2:00 a.m. Those who abused their authority in this manner commanded less respect, but they didn't seem to understand how their overly enthusiastic application of discipline diminished them in the eyes of others.

Around 10:00 one evening, a captain ordered us to remain standing at attention, looking at the fifth floor, arms tight against our sides—until midnight. Standing in one place and not moving for so long was torture, but we made it. Afterward, I fell into bed unconscious. It seemed like only five minutes had passed before it was time to get up again.

We spent Sunday mornings cleaning our dormitory rooms, including waxing the floors and cleaning windows, ceilings, light bulbs, wardrobes—basically everything. The lieutenant or captain used a white glove to check for dust. Usually, the officer would find dust somewhere, in which case we kept cleaning. On Sunday afternoons, they ordered us to do more and more exercises.

Our beds had to be made with the blankets stretched tautly. If the blankets weren't tight enough to bounce a coin, the officers ordered us to do exercises right there between the bunk beds.

We exercised ceaselessly. Our bodies hardened into well-oiled machines, capable of far more than we ever thought possible. The torturous workouts and shared humiliation brought us together, forging bonds of loyalty that would last a lifetime.

The daily routine of life at the detective academy dragged on. The officers never let us forget why we had been selected or what was expected of us. The refrain, usually shouted at us as we stood at attention in the Court of Honor, went something like this:

You were chosen because of your aptitude for leadership, your steadfastness under pressure, and your willingness to take risks when necessary. You will start supervising others next year. But, before that, you must prove that you can follow orders. Don't play games! Don't think you can cut corners! Your life as a cadet will be uncomplicated and safe. Some of you might even think it boring. Your meals might not always be to your liking, but they are nutritious. You have a bed. You have uniforms. You are provided an education. You are provided the means to maintain yourselves in top physical form and are being taught the fundamentals of self-defense and martial arts. In return, you will always conduct yourselves as gentlemen, consistent with the highest code of honor! Soon you will be officers, and much will be expected of you!

The officers also made sure we realized how dangerous our lives would be. They informed us of the constant terrorist attacks targeting policemen.

Once classes started, things fell into a regular schedule. We had to be up at 5:30 a.m., ready for an hour of exercise. After that, we had twenty minutes to shower, make our beds, polish our shoes, dress neatly, comb our hair (even if there wasn't much of it), shave, and straighten the alignment of the bunk beds.

A typical day of cadet training at the detective academy began with everyone standing at attention in formation in the Court of Honor for morning inspection at 6:50. By 7:00, we had breakfast. At 7:40, we ran back to our dormitory rooms— no walking allowed—to brush our teeth and wash our silver-ware. At 7:50, we were back in formation in the Court of Honor, ready to salute the raising of the flag at 8:00.

Classes began at 8:05, and lunch was at noon. At 12:40, we ran back to our dormitory rooms. We had downtime until 1:50, when it was time to go back in formation in the Court of Honor, ready for the start of afternoon classes at 2:05. We were allowed a ten-minute break every hour during the day, but even our breaks were regulated and had to be taken in the Court of Honor.

At 5:50 p.m., classes ended for the day. At 6:00, we were back in formation in the Court of Honor to salute the lowering of the flag. Dinner started at 6:10. We were on our own from 6:40 until 7:50, when we were expected to be back in formation in the Court of Honor for the 8:00 evening inspection. After that, we returned to our classrooms to study until 9:50.

We were expected to be in bed for lights out at 10:00. The only ones up after that were the cadets assigned to guard duty or the cadets being disciplined with additional exercise or ordered to stand at attention for an hour or two in the Court of Honor.

The first-year cadet classes included subjects such as history, typing, criminology, psychology, introduction to constitutional law, introduction to criminal law, introduction to civil procedures, operational rules and procedures, and investigative methods. We also participated in martial arts training a couple of times a week. Occasionally, we competed against other classes in sporting events. Sometimes, one of us challenged a cadet from a higher class to a boxing match, usually a bully we didn't care for.

Every other night, we were assigned a two-hour night patrol. As part of the security procedure at the detective academy, cadets took turns patrolling the facility to guard against attacks. We also stood sentry duty at the main guard hall and in our dormitories. We weren't allowed to make adjustments to our schedule to accommodate night duty. We just had to tough it out.

After five weeks of training with no contact with the outside world, we were finally allowed our first weekend away from the academy. Still, it came with plenty of prohibitions. "Don't get drunk. Don't get into fights. Don't impersonate an officer. Practice safe sex. Do not get into trouble of any kind. If you misbehave and break the gentlemen's code of conduct, you will be expelled!"

As we marched out of the academy that Saturday afternoon for our first free weekend after boot camp, our parents were waiting for us outside. I started to look for my parents, when I saw my dad coming towards me, beaming at me, with Mom right next to him, and a photographer. The three of us posed for a picture. My dad paid the photographer and gave him our address, then we walked to get a taxi to celebrate, having ceviche and a beer before going home. (Ceviche is white fish marinated in freshly squeezed lime juice. Red onions and hot peppers, with a side of boiled, sweet potatoes, complete the dish.) My mom kept beaming at me, not saying much but hugging me every so often and smiling all the time. When the food and drinks came, my dad said, "We are celebrating the fact that my son resisted the five toughest weeks of boot camp as a cadet in an officer school. He is a man now." My dad was usually a discreet man, but on this occasion, he could not resist it. I had very short hair and was wearing my suit, on a bit tight, as I built some more muscles during those weeks. I tried to be serious and calm, but seeing my dad so happy and proud made me very happy. I smiled some.

All I had to do now was to do well in the academy and my parents would be even happier and prouder when I graduated in the next few years.

• Chapter Eight •

TURN OF EVENTS

Once we went back from our first free weekend, everything went back to the rigorous training. We missed even more being free. We had chosen this career, though. Thus we just resigned to endure it. Things went back to normal—very busy with classes and other activities in the academy—except that the killing of military personnel, policemen, and detectives occurred with disturbing regularity. Coffins arrived at our building for viewings and funeral services once a month. On several occasions, I stood guard wearing my dress uniform, positioned respectfully next to the coffin. At these times, I observed the pain and misery of the grieving families—mothers and widows weeping, and colleagues expressing profound grief and rage. The terrible thing was, as the number of assassinations mounted, including detectives we knew, the horror began to feel commonplace, almost normal. Many of us started to talk about it almost casually.

At the end of the year, we took our final examinations. A week later, the detective academy held a graduation ceremony for the cadets who had completed their training. During an afternoon break from the graduation ceremony rehearsal, we were relaxing when one of the fourth-year cadets spotted an officer.

"What is Benedicto doing here?" he murmured in surprise. Then he shouted, "All, attention!"

He ran to stand before the officer and saluted. The officer was a tall, dark man in his early thirties, wearing dark charcoal pants, a silver long-sleeved shirt, and shiny black formal shoes. The officer held a cigarette in one hand and a briefcase in the other. He had broad shoulders, short curly gray hair, and a well-trimmed mustache. He moved like a gladiator with an intelligent, calculating eye. His military bearing was unmistakable. Clearly, he was a man comfortable with the prerogatives of command.

The officer was a captain, and it was evident that the senior cadets knew him and regarded him with admiration and esteem far beyond the customary deference associated with his rank. The captain nodded his head, acknowledging the fourth-year cadet's salute. After he left the area, I asked one of the fourth-year cadets why the captain commanded such respect and reverence.

"Listen, Godson, that captain is Benedicto Jimenez." His words were clipped with impatience, indicating I didn't know anything. "He graduated first in his class from the detective academy. He was the only detective to complete the Peruvian Army Special Forces commando course, and he has led several important busts of criminals, drug dealers, and terrorists. He was also number one in all areas on the performance evaluations for promotion to the next rank. He is a great man with high integrity. We all want to serve under him because it is an honor and privilege, not because we have to." I wondered what it might be like to one day serve under an officer like Captain Jimenez.

The graduation ceremony was held in the Court of Honor, early on a bright summer day, a few days before Christmas. The new lieutenants wore suits, customary for detectives. Proud parents, relatives, and girlfriends were on hand to witness the proceedings, a momentous occasion. The president of Peru and the minister of interior attended, and the director of the Investigation Police officiated. The highlight of the ceremony was the presentation to each honoree of the Silver Insignia of Office by the president of Peru. (The insignia is a badge of authority equivalent to the FBI shield.)

At the ceremony, third-, second-, and first-year cadets stood in formation wearing their dress uniforms. For us, the event concluded with a parade honoring the new lieutenants, while their friends and loved ones applauded and cheered with pride. Then we returned to our dormitory rooms.

After we left, the 200 new lieutenants marched back to the middle of the Court of Honor. The lieutenant who ranked first in his class faced the rest of the honorees, raised his right hand, and shouted, "Break ranks!"

"Long live the detectives!" the new officers shouted back.

The band played festive music appropriate for the joyous occasion, and the new detectives dispersed to find their loved ones. As I stood with my fellow first-year cadets, watching from our fifth-floor dormitory rooms, I remembered the hell the fourth-year cadets—now lieutenants—had given us during our first few weeks at the academy. As difficult as it was, I was happy for the new lieutenants. I certainly respected their accomplishments. I looked forward to the day when I would graduate and celebrate with my family, ready to make my way in the world.

My second year in the academy was almost as busy as the

first year, except that we were not the mangy dogs any longer but the old dogs. Also, coffins arrived at our building for viewings and funeral services more often. It was very hard for my class to learn that among those killings was our godfather, Smiley Eyes, who died as a result of dynamite exploding in his right hand. We kept observing the pain and misery of the grieving families.

The first day we were back from vacation, the alarm bell rang in the middle of the night at the detective academy. Less than two minutes later, my class was standing in formation in the Court of Honor, wearing our khaki uniforms and boots. Captain Benedicto Jimenez had ordered us down, and no one knew why. He told us to get in squat position. We thought he was going to have us do jump squats, but, instead he began to speak. "Gentlemen, the enemy does not sleep. The enemy is always watching. They are waiting for us to lower our guard. The detective must always be alert. We as detectives must observe everybody and everything, but not be obvious about it. Detectives never give up. Detectives solve problems. We must see but never be seen. We cannot afford to be tired. The mind controls the body; the body is just an instrument."

As he talked, Captain Jimenez walked among us with his hands folded behind his back. We forgot our fatigue and listened to the words of this great officer. He didn't shout, just talked to us with his clear, level voice. We listened to him with admiration and respect, his words were rich and powerful. I felt privileged and inspired to be in his presence.

He went on, "We must understand the enemy before we take action against them. We need to understand their motives and strategies. We have to be vigilant or the next victim will be one of us. The terrorists are not rational. They are demented fanatics, like rabid dogs possessed by Satan. When terrorists kill, they shoot you in the back. Then, someone finishes you off with a blow to the head. Explosives will be attached to your body, and you will be blown up so only pieces of your skin or blood will be found on the walls of the nearest building or tree. Only their twisted souls can make them do that to a human being. So, gentlemen, we don't have an option. We must be prepared."

Behind me, one of my promos whispered, "Oh, shit, I can't believe this!"

Captain Jimenez continued. He said we had to believe we would win the war against terrorism and that we had to keep this belief foremost in our minds. He recited some inspirational words to encourage us.

"People can change their lives when they change their attitudes. If you think you will lose, you are probably right. If we think in negative terms, we will obtain negative results. But, if we think in positive terms, we will obtain positive results. Our doubts bring fear. Fear can immobilize us, so we must be confident that we will win. When we have the conviction and determination to win, we are unstoppable. The rest is a matter of hard work and patience."

He concluded his lecture, "So, gentlemen, the terrorists spread chaos and violence wherever they go. If we want to bring peace to our country and change its destiny, we must believe we can do it. However, gentlemen, persistence is critical. As Saint Francis of Assisi said, 'Start by doing what's necessary; then do what's possible, and suddenly you are doing the impossible.' There is only one thing that is certain: The ones who will capture Guzmán and end terrorism in Peru will be the detectives." Captain Jimenez arranged with the academy officials to prominently display positive aphorisms in all classrooms, dormitories, hallways, and even the restrooms, and encouraged us to write them down in our notebooks to remind us of the high ideals we should strive to cultivate in ourselves. This, I knew, would also help me the rest of my life.

In 1990, Captain Jimenez put together a group of

detectives to create the Grupo Especial De Inteligencia— GEIN— (Special Intelligence Group). Its main purpose was to capture the head and other leaders of Shining Path. On September 12, 1992, Abimael Guzmán was captured by then Lieutenant Colonel Benedicto Jimenez. This historical event made it possible to bring peace to Peru, with the hope that the country would have political stability.

During my third year in the academy, in 1985, we were more privileged, less patrolling responsibilities during the week, and only one upper-class cadet picking on us. However, the killings of policemen and military increased. Coffins arrived at our building for viewings and funeral services almost every week as a constant reminder of what was waiting for us out there.

In the middle of the night on March 26, 1985, I was lying in my bunk at the detective academy, wide awake. For no reason I could think of, I felt strangely out of sorts. Someone slipped soundlessly into our dormitory room. He used a pen flashlight to check the names on the bunks. I knew him to be a second-year cadet. Finding my name at the foot of a top bunk, he stopped and, seeing that I was awake, saluted. Whispering softly so as not to disturb the others, he asked me if I was third-year cadet Serván.

"Yes," I answered. "What's up, cadet?"

"Sir, the captain of the day sent me. You are to report to the guard office immediately," he said apologetically.

I was instantly wide awake. Being summoned by an officer in the middle of the night is never good. My first thought was that I must have done something wrong, and now I was about to be punished. I couldn't imagine what I might have done. I told the cadet to let the captain know that I would be right there.

"Yes, sir," he said and saluted again before leaving.

I changed very quickly into my khaki uniform, went down

to the guard office, and reported to the captain of the day.

"Yes, sir," I said, standing at attention and saluting.

"Do you have a brother in the Republican Guard who is a lieutenant?" the captain asked abruptly, without preamble.

That scared me. I thought something horrible must have happened to Edgar.

"Yes, sir," I replied anxiously.

Then he asked me if I knew where he was and where my sisters worked. I answered his questions, wondering where this line of inquiry was going.

"We just got a call a few minutes ago from your house and were given the news that your father suffered a heart attack and died." His voice was impassive, even detached, but I thought I caught a hint of sorrow in his eyes.

"I'm sorry, Serván," he concluded simply.

I didn't react right away. It took a moment or two for the unexpected news to sink in. My first coherent thought was that I had to get home right away. The captain told me that I could take bereavement leave, effective immediately.

It was my sister Monica who had called. She told me later the captain asked several questions to make sure she was my sister. That is why he had asked about Edgar and where my sisters worked.

When I got home, my mom was in total shock, completely unable to cope. My sisters were crying non-stop, not knowing what to do next. It was left to me to take charge. I started by getting the house ready for the viewing. Then I left to complete the paperwork with the Republican Guard for the funeral and burial.

Edgar was working in Tumbes, one of the most remote and inaccessible regions of Peru north of the equator. He wouldn't be able to fly back home until the next morning. The viewing would take place at home the day after that.

Hundreds of people came to show their respects. Papa was

well respected in the community. He spent a great deal of time organizing the neighbors to make San Juan a better place to live.

San Juan is a poor town and lacks many of the services we take for granted in America. It is up to the residents to make the streets safe and the neighborhood a good place to raise a family. Papa was especially good at motivating people to get things done. He organized a fundraising campaign to construct a sidewalk through the neighborhood park. People from the neighborhood took turns keeping the park watered and looking nice.

In San Juan, we knew our neighbors. We cared about and watched out for each other. It was like an extended family. We called our neighborhood a *barrio,* "neighborhood," but in this context, indicating a closeness among the families.

Papa often took time to talk to young kids and teenagers playing or just hanging around the neighborhood. He encouraged them to work hard, respect their parents, help others, and be good citizens. He was a great role model.

My family tried to keep going as before, but it just wasn't possible. We missed Papa too much. He had been our rock, our source of strength and purpose. The world had changed, our rock was gone. In the first few days after his death, we were very sad and worried about how Mama and our younger siblings would survive.

It was a terrible time for all of us. But somehow, we found the strength to go on. We had to, and our grief brought us together. With time comes healing and acceptance. It is the way Papa would have wanted things to be, I know.

Papa was orphaned when he was eight years old. He grew up without parents, living a few months at a time with one or another of his older married sisters or brothers. He told us he didn't want people feeling sorry for us if he died when we were still young.

"My children have to be tough and able to take care of themselves," he would say. "Don't waste time crying. I want you to move on. Work hard and do your best, whatever you do."

The last time I saw Papa alive was the previous Sunday. Before I left for the detective academy, Papa said, "Use good judgment in life, and don't be overly critical of others. Keep in mind the character of a man is not measured by how many times he falls, but by how many times he gets up again and keeps going." It is the last thing I remember him telling me.

Papa's death was devastating for me and the entire family, but Papa expected us to keep going and to make something of our lives.

In 1986, when I was already a fourth-year cadet, at a New Year neighborhood party, I saw Mary, the girl I liked in high school. Mary and I danced and had a good time. She was flirting with me, and I liked that. At one point, she even rested her head on my chest, and I felt that old electric shiver of delight running through me. Then she looked up at me and smiled, and I smiled back. After I learned that she was not dating anyone, I considered the possibility of dating Mary. After all, I liked her in high school, and I was attracted to her now.

Peru elected a new president the previous year, Alan Garcia, who announced the unification of the three police forces into one in 1986. Terrorism intensified, the economy worsened, and unemployment rose ever higher. The government now wanted to use any new buildings for their new political agenda. As a result, all the cadets from the detective academy were ordered to move in March 1986 to an unfinished school around thirteen miles east of Lima. There, we had no water or electricity.

Fourth-year cadets had to select special training that would determine the course of their careers after graduation.

I knew that I wanted to serve with either the antiterrorist division or anti-drug/anti-organized crime division, but I hadn't made up my mind yet.

A few days before the move to Barbadillo Estate, Mary and I began dating and I felt very good about it; I even thought about proposing to her by the time of my graduation.

We were busy packing and moving everything from Surquillo to our new home, leaving behind many good memories. After the move, the first few days were occupied with physical fitness training. We trained on the obstacle course, ran miles up and down the hills, and patrolled the grounds in addition to our regular schedule of classes.

I finally decided to train for service in the antiterrorist division after graduation. I also thought I would study for a law degree. A degree in law in Peru can be very helpful for those interested in higher management. I could definitely see myself rising to the level of general by the time I was 44.

My future was well-planned. It would take a lot of hard work, but the way was clear. I would become a detective—young, determined, ambitious—someone willing to fight to bring peace to society. What I didn't know then was that I was about to experience yet another turn of events that would dramatically change my destiny.

• Chapter Nine •

AFTER THE EXPLOSION

When the grenade exploded, at first, I felt no pain. Time slowed, and I felt myself detach from my own body, traveling quietly but quite rapidly through a dark tunnel of clouds. Far away, I could see a white light. I remember thinking, "Oh shit, I'm dead!" I thought of my mother, my younger brothers and sisters, the recent passing of our father—and I realized one more death would devastate my family.

"I don't want to die," I told God. Immediately, the dark-cloud tunnel that had appeared in front of me vanished, and I again felt the ground beneath me. I staggered as I tried to stand, cursing my destiny—the bursting noise, the tearing fragments, the blinding flash. Intense pain from my ears coursed through my upper body, enveloping my face.

My training at the detective academy included protocols for such situations. I remembered that, many times, what kills is the noise; the sudden increase in pressure from a blast wave can destroy eardrums, lungs, and other pressure-sensitive internal organs. Our instructors taught us that if we found ourselves reeling from a nearby explosion, we should lie down and keep our mouths open. That is what I did and then felt the cold, firm ground under me.

I could hear my partner Jesús's terrified voice crying for help. Bursts of machine gun fire erupted from the hilltops all around the police school, the explosion having provoked fire from the cadets on vice patrol to discourage any potential attack.

Jesús continued to shout and call for help, but it seemed as if no one was listening. Or perhaps they couldn't hear us; we were positioned about 400 meters away from the instructional classroom area and the Court of Honor.

My left arm throbbed from severe pain, and my right arm seemed to not exist. The funeral of Lieutenant Pedro Vasquez Benítez, Smiley Eyes, came to mind. Two years earlier, a dynamite stick had exploded in his right hand, blowing his right arm entirely off, along with half of his face. He died immediately. Wax moldings of his face and arm had been created to make him look more natural in his coffin. The contrast between artificial and real skin color was ghastly. A yellowish liquid oozed from the seams where wax met flesh, and the wax hand that extended from his sleeve had no pores or hairs to make it more lifelike.

A thick, warm liquid ran down my face, arms, and abdomen. It had to be blood. I didn't know if it was coming from internal injuries or exterior wounds, but I knew my right side was bleeding heavily. If I still had an arm, the blood might have been coming from my shoulder, my elbow, or my wrist— I simply didn't know. I couldn't open my eyes. They hurt intensely, and the pain in my eyes and body compelled me to lie still where I was on the ground.

"Carlos, can you hear me?" Jesús yelled. "Oh, God. Carlos, can you hear me?" He sounded desperate and really scared, but I couldn't respond. The all-consuming pain in my head and face was too great for me to speak. In fact, the pain and intense ringing in my ears made it hard to even think. All I could do was keep still and hope that I wasn't too badly hurt inside.

As time passed, Jesús grew more distressed. He wanted me to move any part of my body to let him know that I could still hear and understand what he was saying. He needed to know if I were still connected with reality.

I thought about moving my arms or head, but the pain led me to quickly reject that idea. Jesús did not give up. He implored me to do something. It was all I could do to move my right foot from side to side. Relieved, Jesús touched my left shoulder gently, signaling me to remain still. He shouted loudly at cadets rushing toward us to get the ambulance. Then he spoke to me, reassuring me that help was on the way. A doctor was always on call, and a gutted ambulance was parked near the police school's nursing office.

I felt the sun going down on my face and smelled the distinct scent of soil and blood. I thought that perhaps the soil was absorbing my blood. I don't know why, but I saw this as evidence that I wasn't dead. I listened to Jesús's incessant chatter as he tried to maintain his connection with me as time crawled by. My eyes, face, and abdomen had been severely injured, and, as great as the pain had been initially, it only became progressively more and more intense. Meanwhile, my lifeblood continued to flow.

I heard the engine of an approaching vehicle. Relieved, I knew it had to be the ambulance bringing the doctor, anesthesia, emergency supplies, and whatever else was needed to stop the bleeding and treat my wounds.

Then Jesús shouted, "Where's the ambulance?"

Two cadets, Esquerre Nunez and Tumi Cordova yelled

back, "The ambulance can't make it up the hill. They're send-ing a garbage truck."

Tumi and Esquerre ran up to Jesús, and the three of them lifted me into the smelly garbage truck with great care. Over and over, they said, "Take it easy, promo."

By now, I imagined half an hour or more had passed since the explosion, but, in fact, only around three minutes had gone by. As the heavy garbage truck started back, my classmates urged the driver to go faster down the rough and narrow road. At the detective academy parking lot, the ambulance was waiting and ready to go with its engine on.

Again, cadets carefully lifted me down from the garbage truck. I thought I would be placed on a stretcher and medical personnel would connect me to equipment to monitor my vital signs. That didn't happen. Instead, I found myself on the cold aluminum floor of the ambulance. No stretcher, anesthesia, fluids, alcohol, or any other disinfectant. No cotton or gauze—nothing! I couldn't understand why they didn't have the necessary supplies and equipment you see in the movies.

Every bump on the rough road sent severe pain shooting through my head and back. I could hear how the doctor removed one of his shoelaces to make a tourniquet for my right arm. Severe pain shot up and down both of my arms, and the ringing in my ears was so loud I could not speak.

"Hang in there, promo. Stay with us. We are already on our way to the hospital," one of my classmates said. He gently placed his folded jacket under my head for a pillow.

The doctor and my two classmates, Tumi and Esquerre, squatted the entire time (Jesús stayed at the school because he had to report what had happened.) The ambulance had no chairs or benches. I think someone sat on the metal inner fender above one of the rear wheels.

I heard someone ask, "Is he going to make it, Doctor?"

"No," the doctor answered sadly, but with conviction.

What's this? Were they talking about my arm, my eyes, or, worse, my chances of living? Never mind, I thought. I couldn't worry about it. The incredible pain, especially in my abdomen, fully occupied my attention. I was still bleeding, and every jarring bump on the road made it worse.

The ambulance had to go slowly, as we passed through a very bumpy area with unpaved roads, heavy with the smell of farmland and cattle. After several minutes, we pulled onto the main road, Carretera Central. The driver turned left, heading west. He immediately picked up speed, but only for a few minutes. Traffic was at its peak. The roads were crowded with trucks bringing produce from the Andes, buses, and cars, all trying to get ahead of one another.

I couldn't understand why we weren't getting through. Didn't people know that this was an emergency? Then I realized that the ambulance siren was off. "Why doesn't the driver turn on the siren?" I wondered.

Tumi must have had the same thought. He shouted through the window in the partition, "Turn on the siren!"

"I can't. It doesn't work!" the driver shouted back.

Esquerre asked the doctor if I were going to need a blood transfusion. "Yes," the doctor said.

"As soon as we get to the hospital, Carlos can have my blood," Tumi said.

Esquerre said that he would donate blood as well. This made me feel better, knowing that my friends were willing to do anything for me.

Blocked by traffic, the ambulance could barely move, so Tumi and Esquerre leaned heads and shoulders out the back door, shouting to drivers to clear a way for the ambulance. One of them climbed out in frustration and got in front with the ambulance driver. They both blew their police whistles with no effect. Then they started firing their guns into the air. That did the trick. The other drivers were finally convinced to make way for the ambulance, and we began moving faster.

Hermilio Valdizan Hospital was on Carretera Central, just two or three miles from the detective school. Apparently, we went right past it.

"Why didn't we turn in to the hospital?" Esquerre seemed confused.

"We have to go to the police hospital," the driver and the doctor responded at the same time.

I really could not believe this. At a time like this, adhering to protocols seemed crazy. I might very well die because of some kind of stupid procedural requirement.

Tumi and Esquerre and the driver eventually ran out of ammunition and our progress was once again reduced to a crawl. The engines and horns from hundreds of vehicles could be heard all around us. My friends went back to ineffectually shouting and blowing their whistles.

I began feeling despair. I knew it was critical for me to stay conscious. If I passed out, I was afraid I might suffer brain damage or, worse, I might never wake up. Somewhere before, I was sure I heard that traumatic brain injury was more likely if a person loses consciousness after a serious head injury. Several miles later, I could hear familiar noises—conductors from buses announcing their routes and a few frustrated drivers blowing their horns. I could also smell the odor of garbage and, at times, I got a whiff of sewer water.

At last, we began moving faster, then faster still. In the ambulance, my classmates had stopped speaking to me. Perhaps they thought I lost consciousness. Finally, after what seemed like a long time, we pulled up in front of the police hospital's emergency door. This time there was a stretcher. I couldn't feel the sun anymore, and the air felt light and cool. I suspected it was probably getting late in the day.

A few news reporters came out when the ambulance drove up. When they saw my body, they wanted to know if I were still alive. No one answered their questions. Everyone was focused on helping the nurses as hospital personnel gently moved me onto a hospital stretcher. As the medical staff worked on me, someone pushed them aside all at once, and the journalists took pictures of my body.

One journalist touched my left shoulder and asked, "What happened? Who did this?"

That was enough for Tumi. He pushed the journalist back and shouted, "Get out of here, you son of a bitch!"

The nurses quickly moved my stretcher to the emergency room and closed the door behind us. Tumi and Esquerre left my side to donate blood. When I reached the operating room, I was moved onto a table. The strong scent of antiseptics filled my nostrils. Everything was happening very rapidly now.

"Call the orthopedist, call the ophthalmologist, get the doctor on duty, call the nurses, and hurry up, dammit!" someone shouted. After a few minutes, a doctor arrived and took control, giving instructions in a calm, authoritative voice.

One of the nurses said, "The doctor from the police school said it was a grenade explosion."

"Shit! Thank God he's alive," the doctor said.

Nurses opened my shirt and cut off my undershirt. I heard small tables being moved close to the operating table and the metallic sound of medical instruments being prepared for use. Everyone followed the doctor's instructions carefully.

"Hurry! This cadet has lost a lot of blood! We need to give him a blood transfusion! Get someone from the lab right away! We need to know his blood type!" The doctor continued to bark out orders with authority.

"B positive," I said calmly, finally able to speak, fully lucid.

All activity came to a grinding halt. Someone touched my head. A startled nurse said, "He's conscious!"

"Can you hear me okay?" the doctor asked.

"Yes," I answered.

"What is your name?"

"Fourth-year cadet Serván Triveño, Carlos Rigoberto."

Three doctors worked on me at the same time, using surgical pliers and tweezers to remove the metal shrapnel from my body. One doctor worked on my left arm, the second on my right arm, and the third on my abdomen. The third doctor observed that the abdominal muscles were strong enough to prevent shrapnel from penetrating my body. Each time they removed a piece of metal, they opened a new wound, causing more bleeding. The excruciating pain nearly made me pass out; however, I maintained my resolve to stay awake. The metal fragments were of different shapes and sizes. All had sharp, jagged edges. It was like a carpenter removing nails from a piece of wood. The shrapnel had to be pulled from my skin and from deep in my muscles. I had never felt so much pain. It felt as if they were tearing flesh and bones from my body. All I could do was close my eyes tightly and clench my teeth as they went about their work. After a few minutes, one of the doctors removed a large piece of metal deeply embedded in the muscle of my left hand. With a great sense of relief, the pain disappeared, and I finally lost consciousness.

When I awoke, I had no idea what time it was. My eyes were covered, and everything was dark. I heard a radio softly playing romantic music and smelled the familiar, comforting aroma of fresh coffee. I could hear two young women nearby quietly discussing their duties. I could feel that my left arm was connected to some kind of medical device. I tried to move my arms, but it was very painful. Remembering the explosion, I started to do an inventory of my body in my head. I was able to feel and move my legs, I was able to feel my stomach without pain (no internal damage there), I felt my arms but could not move them, I could hear well, I could think, I did not feel pain in my eyes but could not see anything. Then I wondered about the condition of my arms and eyes. I should just wait for the doctors to talk to me, I thought, fearing very bad news.

"Where am I? Who are you?" I asked politely, despite my pain.

"You're in the intensive care unit at the police hospital, and we are nurses," a friendly voice answered.

"That coffee smells wonderful. Could I please have a cup?"

One of the young nurses told me, "I will give you a cup, even though the coffee is really for the nurses, not the patients."

Her tone of voice told me that she was smiling. They checked my vital signs, and we chatted for a while before I fell back asleep.

When I woke up again, one of the nurses asked if I felt well enough to have a couple of visitors—my brother and sister.

"Of course, I want to see them." It would be the first time I had seen a member of my family since the explosion. I wondered how they had learned about the accident and how my mother was taking the news.

Two people came in. My sister Monica gasped and exclaimed, "Your face!" She sounded like she was about to cry.

Edgar, my eldest brother, didn't really know what to say. He asked awkwardly, feigning calmness, "How are you doing, Bro?"

"I'm doing okay, but how are Mama, Ernesto, and Gloria?" Ernesto and Gloria, the youngest members of the family, were only six and four years old at the time.

Monica lightly touched my left shoulder. I could feel her hand trembling. Every few seconds, she absentmindedly pressed her nails into my skin. Neither Monica nor Edgar brought up my medical condition, and I didn't ask. I was afraid to, even though I knew that eventually I would have to face the truth. The news couldn't be good. All I could do was stay calm and deal with it as best I could.

It would be six months before Monica could tell me what happened to them that day.

She explained, "It was April first. That evening, when I got home from work and saw the door open with the lights on, I knew something was very wrong. Several of our neighbors were looking at our house from their windows or open doors. I checked to make sure no one was inside the house. Then I saw Constance from four doors down walking toward me. Her face said it all—bad news, and a chill ran right through me. I flashed back to the day last year when Papa died. I missed him so much. Constance told me that you had suffered a horrible accident. I immediately thought the worst. Desperate, I asked her where you were. She told me you were at the police hospital and the rest of the family had gone to be with you— except Ernesto and Gloria, who were staying with the neighbors next door.

"I ran to the next street to find a taxi. When I arrived at the hospital, I saw some of our cousins and aunts. Their faces bore expressions like the day of our father's funeral. Mama couldn't stop crying, and no one knew details about your condition. When I heard you had picked up an explosive that detonated, I thought you were dead. Edgar stood by the stairs, his hands covering his face." Monica said that when she walked up to Edgar, he was distraught.

"Why? Why did this have to happen to Carlos? He is always joking, very active, and responsible. It should have happened to me."

Monica went on, "Edgar scared the hell out of me. He was talking like you were dead, and Aunt Natalia and Cousin Tereza had tears in their eyes. It was like Dad's funeral all over again."

Early the next morning, I was transferred to the recovery floor of the officers clinic. After a check of my vital signs, a nurse brought me a big bowl of oatmeal with milk. I could not move my arms, so the head nurse fed me. When she saw how ravenously I ate, she ordered two more bowls of oatmeal brought in. After that, I had three ham sandwiches on multigrain bread. I hadn't had dinner the previous night, and my empty stomach burned with hunger. The nurse adjusted my bed so I could rest with my back at a 45-degree angle. Then she put a pillow under my head and another under my right arm. It seemed strange that she did not put a pillow under my left arm. Neither the doctor nor the nurses told me anything about my medical and physical condition. And, fearing the worst, I did not want to ask.

Listening to the news on the radio, I knew it was around 9:00 a.m. when my mother came in. She touched my left foot. Then she stepped closer and kissed my forehead because the rest of my face was covered in gauze. The doctor had ordered the nurses to apply the burn medication and leave the gauze exposed. I noticed that my mother was forcing herself to sound calm and cheerful as she told me that they were making every effort to transfer me to a hospital that specialized in eye surgery. That statement confirmed my fear that my eyes had been badly damaged, but I was confident that the doctors and advanced technology would be able to handle my situation just fine.

A couple of days passed, and over the weekend many people came to visit. Neighbors and friends from elementary school, middle school, high school, and the detective academy all came. Relatives, family members, and, of course, my girlfriend, Mary, were there to encourage and support me. Having so many people caring for me was truly touching, though a bit overwhelming. Every day, groups of people came to visit—so many that the nurses would come to my room to tell people their time was up so the next group could come in. The support they gave me was so important that it's still difficult for me to describe just how much it meant. Suffice it to say that their presence gave me hope and encouragement.

• Chapter Ten •

SUSPENSE IN THE MIDDLE OF THE NIGHT

I found it nearly impossible to sleep during the first few weeks after my accident. Despite the strong medication, I experienced constant, tremendous pain in my arm. I especially worried about my right arm—because of the pain and because the nurses were always careful to keep it resting on a pillow.

I also considered the horrible possibility that I no longer had a right hand, although I was sure I could still feel it. The pain proved that the hand was still there, didn't it? That hand couldn't be gone. It just couldn't. Even though I couldn't move it, the hand had to be there.

The terrible possibility consumed me. My arm had been badly injured, but no one talked about it. Not to me, anyway. The only way for me to assess the damage, since I couldn't see for myself, was to touch my right arm with my left hand. I quickly found out that wasn't such an easy thing to do.

Incredible bolts of pain shot through my arm and upper body every time I tried to move my left arm. The joints of my shoulder and elbow felt frozen in place. The effort drained me physically. Even so, I refused to let this defeat me.

Every night, I renewed my effort, determined to move my arm a bit more towards the right side of my body. Eventually, I would get there, and any fears I had for my right hand could be put to rest. That was my hope. That's what I kept telling myself.

The sounds of the night could be heard from my window, the familiar blaring of car horns at a distance and the peculiar chirping of crickets behind the building. Soft, romantic music played at the nurse's station. I could hear my two sleeping roommates breathing heavily. My left hand made soft rustling sounds as it moved painfully across the blanket toward my right arm. I reached my abdomen, took a deep breath, and paused briefly to regroup.

I shifted my head towards my right arm, drew in another deep breath, and started again. Several long, painful, interminable minutes later, my left hand stretched across to the right side of my waist. At this point, my left elbow and shoulder felt like they had loosened up and could move with greater ease.

"A little bit more, a bit more," I repeated to myself as I struggled to push my left hand to meet its partner. Though my shoulder throbbed, I wasn't going to stop now.

"Keep going, Carlos. Almost there." I urged myself on.

Then I touched the gauze at the end of my right arm. Now I knew the awful truth. Any sense of triumph I might have felt about this physical achievement immediately vanished with a crushing blow. There was nothing there. It felt like a small fist wrapped in bandages. The breath left my body, and my left arm fell back to my left side. My worst fears were realized. I no longer had a right hand! A devastating wave of powerful emotions swept over me. I felt tremendous loss, uncertainty, and shock. How could I possibly deal with this?

All alone, in the middle of the night, I forced myself to get a grip on my crashing emotions. I calmed myself down and began to think through things logically and rationally.

"It is better this way—that I'm alone. I'm a cool-headed guy who solves his own problems, and that is what I need to do now," I reasoned.

My thoughts strayed to the ludicrous. I would no longer be able to give a proper military salute to my superiors. "What a silly idea, Carlos." I chuckled to myself.

I had to consider how I would get along without my right hand. It had been my dominant hand—the one that I punched with in karate lessons, the hand I drew with, the hand I wrote with, the one I used to eat, and so on. I had much to come to terms with, but I realized that I would gain nothing by lamenting or feeling sorry for myself. I did not allow myself to feel depressed. I did not cry. On the contrary, strangely, it gave me a boost of courage to face the challenge. All through this process, I felt thankful to even be alive. My brain wasn't damaged, my hearing still worked well, and the rest of my body was in good condition, at least for now.

I would learn later that the feeling of still having my missing hand was known as phantom limb syndrome. People who suffer from this disorder feel sensations and even pain in a limb that no longer exists.

I spent the rest of that night thinking about how I might do things with only one hand. I remembered a woman who sold flowers by the stadium. Mama frequented her stand to buy flowers to take to the cemetery. The woman did not have legs, but she used her strong arms and hands to move about. She supported her small body on her partially exposed buttocks, dirty and calloused from constant friction with the floor. She smiled as she sold her flowers, and she showed no concern for her physical condition or the exposure of a normally private portion of her body. Though she had limited physical ability, her spirit and her resolve remained strong. I realized that I, too, could adjust to the loss of my right hand and be as normal and productive as anybody else.

In Peru, our sense of humor is many times sardonic. The next morning, my brother-in-law Augusto came to visit. As we talked, I began making jokes about my missing hand. His somber tone quickly changed to excitement and obvious surprise. He said that everyone had been afraid that I was not yet emotionally ready to accept the loss of my hand. For sure, nobody wanted to be the one to tell me. They all thought the news would over-whelm me, and I might become depressed. I told him that I thought I had lost my entire arm, and I was happy to discover it was only my hand. Augusto seemed relieved by my positive attitude.

Mama arrived a few minutes later that morning, and Augusto was quick to tell her that I knew that my right hand was gone and that I was handling the situation better than most people. She stood next to my bed and exclaimed proudly and cheerfully, "Oh, my son!" Then she kissed my forehead. From that point on, some of my friends and relatives felt comfortable talking and even joking about my missing hand. I would observe similar reactions frequently after that. The degree to which people are comfortable around individuals with disabilities often reflects the degree to which those individuals with disabilities feel comfortable in their own skins.

After days of tests and meetings, my doctor told me the police hospital did not have a retina specialist, or the updated medical equipment needed to perform the specialized eye surgery. He and his team decided to transfer me to the Santo Toribio de Mogrovejo Hospital in Lima for further treatment. I faced the very real possibility that I might be blind, but I resolved to set aside my fears and place my trust and faith in the doctors.

Santo Toribio de Mogrovejo Hospital was an extension of a nunnery that tended to the most needy and impoverished. One giant room housed all the forty or so beds. Two guards from the penitentiary stayed by my bed guarding a criminal named Eduardo who, according to the nurses, was at risk of losing both eyes from injuries resulting from a terrible prison fight.

In spite of the austere conditions, the care was good. The doctors and nurses worked carefully and gently each morning as they tended my wounds. The day after I arrived, a nurse took me to see Dr. Herrera, a nationally recognized retina specialist. I had much hope when we entered his office. However, he never once spoke to me as he examined my eyes.

"The right eye is gone," said the doctor indifferently, as if he were speaking of a bad piece of meat. "There is a chance with the left eye. Let's schedule the surgery for tomorrow, first thing in the morning." Ignoring me completely, Dr. Herrera turned to his assistant and said, "Next patient."

After the surgery, I had to lie face down to help the retina attach and heal properly. To lie face down for hours and hours was very uncomfortable, but I had no choice; I simply had to deal with it.

The day following my surgery, another doctor worked on my arms and abdomen, cleaning my wounds and checking for infections. Then a nurse took me in a wheelchair back to Dr. Herrera's office so he could evaluate my left eye and tell me the results of the surgery. He did not greet me, not even a simple "hello." In a rushed manner, he removed the bandages and placed my cheek against some kind of examination device to look at my eye. I sat there waiting, expectant and hopeful. For a few minutes, he looked through the examination instrument without speaking. Finally, he said, "This eye is also gone.

Next patient." He spoke with the same abrupt, unsympathetic tone he used at our first meeting. The nurse said nothing, placed a new bandage on my eye, and wheeled me back to my bed. The doctor's indifference left me feeling cold.

On the way back to my hospital room, the stunning implications of the doctor's pronouncement slowly sunk in. Once in my bed, I thought more about what it all meant. Missing one hand and having lost one eye was one thing; being completely blind on top of losing my right hand was a whole different deal. I did not know what to say or how to react. I could feel my positive attitude and toughness melting away.

That afternoon, Uncle Rigoberto, Papa's older brother and a general with the Police Investigation Department, stopped by to check on my progress. With a knot in my throat, my guts tight, and tears in my eyes, I said, "The doctor just told me that I will not be able to see."

My uncle gently touched my right shoulder and spoke in a soothing voice, "It is okay, son. We are working on getting things arranged so you can go to the United States. Their eye surgeons are doing amazing things there. They have very advanced medical procedures, and I'm certain things will be okay."

Uncle Rigoberto left to talk to the doctors. I calmed myself and thought about my situation and what the future might bring. What had happened was far more serious than I had initially thought. I also remembered that a few days earlier, a couple of officers came from the academy to check my status and to let me know that an explosives specialist found more booby traps on those two mountains. They maybe thought that such news was reassuring, but if something like this was happening to me, I wanted it to be when I had a chance to fire back. It made me angry. However, just like when I faced the loss of my hand, I reminded myself that I was still alive, and my mind was working fine, as was most of my body. So, with renewed determination, I again resolved to meet the future with courage and hope. I realized I needed to be prepared for the challenges that lay ahead and be ready to face my future as a man.

"After all," I assured myself, "those who are willing to give their lives to protect others have to be prepared and tough—not just when fighting against terrorists and criminals, but also when facing life's challenges."

Back at the police hospital, Uncle Rigoberto and my mother put as much pressure on the staff as possible so paperwork and red tape would not delay my departure for the United States. The Minister of Interior had an agreement with the Johns Hopkins Hospital, so that is where my surgery would take place. Again, I felt hopeful. I thought I would regain my vision and be fitted with a well-functioning prosthetic right hand. After all, I was going to the most powerful country in the world with the most advanced science and technology, so my prospects seemed good. Still, I worried and suffered from anxiety. The days passed faster and faster. I knew my classmates were moving on without me, and the fear I might never graduate robbed me of sleep. Though I didn't realize it at the time, I was in some kind of denial.

One sleepless night, I smelled something bad, like over-full dumpsters or piles of garbage. The horrible stench filled my nostrils and I couldn't escape it. Earlier in the day, I remembered that a friend complained of a bad odor in my room. I told her that it was probably the garbage behind the building. She looked out the windows but saw nothing that might be causing the smell. Now, lying there in my bed, I thought about what the problem might be. When I thought about it, I realized that I had never heard garbage trucks behind this building or the sound of people throwing garbage into a dumpster.

"That's not normal," I reasoned. "Hospital rooms do not smell like this."

Using my sense of smell like a dog sniffing around for food, it came to me that the smell might actually be somewhere in my room, not outside. I turned my head to the left. No smell. Then I turned to my right. The foul odor was stronger. I became very alarmed, thinking someone might have left garbage under my bed. The smell came from my right. I wanted to know if it was coming from near my head or my feet. I began to quietly sniff around. I did not want to disturb anyone. I could hear soft music coming from the nursing station, the snores of one of my roommates, and distant traffic noises. Moving my head ever closer to my right arm, I was shocked and terrified when I realized that the horrible odor was coming from the end of my arm.

I couldn't believe it! My arm was the source of that horrific odor!

My frustration grew as I recounted my care in that hospital. Early the next morning, I let the doctor have the full force of my anger. "Since I came here from the Santo Toribio de Mogrovejo Hospital two weeks ago, my bandages have not been changed. I am literally decomposing right here in a hospital!"

Without responding, the doctor turned away and ordered the nurses to attend to my wounds. As the nurses removed the bandages, the foul odor grew worse. Fortunately, my wounds weren't infected, but the nurses jerked the bandages off as if they were simply removing a tablecloth from a table, showing no concern for my comfort. Then they hurriedly cleaned and disinfected my wounds. The pain was so intense that I thought perhaps they were retaliating because I complained. I was afraid that my wounds would start bleeding again, adding even more pain and stress to an already painful and stressful experience. From then on, each morning the nurses attended to my wounds—cleaning them, checking them for signs of infection, and bandaging them again.

My days were a blur of physical discomfort, brief periods of conversation with family and friends, and extended periods of boredom. I had plenty of time to mull things over and worry about what the future might have in store. I was still planning on graduation from the detective academy at the end of the year and was concerned about falling further and further behind in my studies. My only hope rested on doctors and a hospital in the United States whose advanced medical technology might be able to restore my sight and make me an artificial hand to replace some of the ability I had lost.

I counted down the hours until I could travel to the United States. While I spent time with my visitors, Mama and Uncle Rigoberto labored to finish the necessary paperwork. Although I was excited about the possibility of being treated by doctors in the United States, I also worried about how I would manage in a new country—a country with a language I did not know and unfamiliar customs. I had so much to think about.

● Chapter Eleven ●

RETURN TO LIMA

In early May 1986, Mama and I traveled to Johns Hopkins Hospital in Baltimore for surgery on both eyes. A brother of a classmate from the detective academy generously opened his home to us while we were there.

We were told that surgery on the left eye had been successful, but the right eye could not be saved. The damage to that eye had been too great. Mama was also able to use money from the sale of a family truck to purchase a prosthesis for my missing right hand. The Peruvian government did not give us a check for the prosthesis, as Peru has very limited resources; the eye surgery was the priority. After nearly three months, we were told that, medically, they could not do anything else for me. It was time for me to go home.

My classmate's brother encouraged me to stay in America where the full range of services for the blind was so much better than anything available in Peru, but I wasn't ready for that yet. I still believed my vision would be totally restored and I could graduate with my class at the detective academy in December.

I thought I had reason to hope. After all, my vision gradually improved. At first, I could only tell light from dark. Then I was able to make out shadows and movement. Finally, I could distinguish bright colors. This was far from any kind of functional vision, but I had to believe that full sight would be restored. Clearly, I was in denial.

Mama and I landed in Lima on a dark, misty afternoon in August, and, despite my feelings of uncertainty, it felt good to be home. I wrapped my arm around Mama's shoulders as we came down the stairs. A light mist touched my face, and my muscles tightened at the midwinter chill. A police hospital ambulance sat on the nearby tarmac where my family waited to welcome us. We had come home!

I will always have fond memories of how my little six-year-old brother, Ernesto, shouted out my name and ran to hug my waist. I had to bend my knees to give him a good hug. Then my little four-year-old sister, Gloria, also ran up and gave me a hug.

Gloria touched my prosthetic hand and, in a disappointed voice, exclaimed, "This is a plastic hand, like the ones dolls have!"

My prosthesis made some of the people around us uncomfortable, and Mama told Gloria to stop talking about my hand, but I couldn't help smiling. It filled my heart with joy to hear my four-year-old sister's candid and concerned voice. I was with my family again, and it felt good to be home!

We decided not to take the ambulance to the police hospital. After all, the medical exams and reports could wait a couple of days. I had been away for almost three months and wanted to enjoy time at home with my family and, of course, time with my girlfriend, Mary.

Mama talked about the differences between the US and Peru on our way home. She commented on how clean the streets of Baltimore and Arlington were compared to the streets of Lima. The air pollution in Lima is oppressive, and garbage would be seen piled high wherever you went. Children were often seen begging for money or trying to sell whatever small items they could. Abject poverty was so much more obvious here. Still, we were happy to be back in our own country.

At first, all seemed to be going well. I enjoyed visits from friends and relatives. I especially enjoyed being reunited with my girlfriend. Then things began to change. It became clear that I would not graduate with my class from the detective academy, and my vision wasn't improving.

On top of everything else, my doctors ordered a protracted period of bed rest to facilitate my recovery. Home confinement and inactivity were not just difficult, they were frightening. I wanted to believe that I had a future bright with promise, that I had goals to achieve. I could not conceive of a life of dependency on others.

What would I do now? I would never become a police detective. I knew that now. I also knew that I couldn't resign myself to a future of inactivity and helplessness either. I had to find a way forward, but how? What can I become, and how can I make it happen? I was floundering and needed help.

Every time I went back to the police hospital for monitoring, the doctors told me the same thing. My condition was unchanged. I found that answer unsatisfactory. I didn't want to know only where I was at that moment. I needed to know what my prospects were. I went to the Santo Toribio de Mogrovejo Hospital for a second opinion. There, Dr. Herrera saw me again and reviewed my medical records. He said that he could not really do anything more for me other than what had already been done. He also said that I needed to allow more time for my recovery, but I was already reaching the conclusion that more time would not make any difference.

I began to experience sharp pain in my right eye, which only got worse as the months went by. The eye was also shrinking and showing signs of infection. The doctors from the Mogrovejo Hospital recommended that my right eye be removed. Otherwise, the infection could spread and damage the left eye. I didn't want to do it, but I felt like I had no choice. A few days later, I was lying on an operating table waiting for my right eye to be removed.

The doctor injected a local anesthetic directly into my right eyeball. I winced and arched my back in pain. The anesthetic took hold, and the operation began. I remained conscious throughout the procedure. Later, they described the procedure this way: Muscles, nerves, and blood vessels within the eye socket were cut, and blood streamed down the right side of my face. A nurse kept wiping away excess blood. The terrifying surgical experience reminded me of the trauma of that fateful day of my accident outside the detective academy. I thought I had prepared mentally for the thirty-minute procedure, but it was still deeply disturbing.

Thoughts swirled around in my head. No longer would people just notice my missing hand, they would also notice my missing eye. What will people think? Will they pity me? I couldn't allow myself to dwell on that. I couldn't give in to self-pity. Keep moving forward. That was the only way.

Someone from the hospital told me about a dentist who made prosthetic eyes and ears, so I made an appointment. He crafted an artificial eye from acrylics, complete with an artfully painted iris and veins. His staff told me that, at first glance, the prosthesis looked real, but upon closer examination, people would be able to tell it was artificial.

I had to figure out how to deal with my new situation. The

way my family came together to support me was gratifying. They were quick to help in every way possible whenever they could, but I had to learn how to do things for myself. Learning to manage with only one hand while, at the same time, learning how to function without sight, proved to be complicated. I had been right-handed, so using my left hand for everything was awkward. At first, I frequently dropped things and reflexively would try to use my missing right hand to catch or steady the item. When the object inevitably fell, I became frustrated. This happened with my food, clothing, soap, silverware, plates, cups, glasses, razors, belt, pillowcases, the broom, and so on. Sometimes I just had to step away, but I always came back and tried again. I would take a deep breath, count to ten, then examine the object carefully with my hand. Slowly, I figured out better ways to hold things and developed the coordination to manipulate each object successfully.

Going on a walk with one of my brothers or sisters, I occasionally stumbled, and, as I fell forward, I would reflectively throw my hands in front of me to protect myself. Striking the ground, my right arm would hurt like hell! No muscles protected the area of my amputation to provide some cushion for the bones, as my hand once did. The reality of that permanent injury was terribly frustrating and very painful. Even worse, it was humiliating, knowing that people were watching and feeling sorry for me.

Still, I longed to be independent again. With a great deal of practice and determination, I learned to do many things for myself. One of the most complicated and challenging tasks I faced was learning to tie my shoes with one hand.

During this time, I had a continuous stream of visitors. In addition to friends and relatives, classmates from the detective academy came and offered their heartfelt support. I was grateful for their friendship and concern, but I ached with sadness, knowing that I would not be graduating with them.

On a warm, sunny afternoon in October, I went back to the detective academy to get my belongings. The major in charge was amiable, and he notified the brigade leader that I had arrived. Marco Palomino accompanied me as I collected my stuff. Then the fourth-year cadets were ordered into formation on the parade ground so I could speak to them. I knew this would be the last time I would get to talk to all my classmates at once. I did not want them to feel sorry for me.

Mustering the most positive attitude I could, I said, "As long as someone is alive, there is hope to be independent and productive. One always must continue fighting and never give up on this long and challenging journey. I know that I can count on any and all of you if I ever need help. I also know that I will be facing many obstacles, but I am ready for the fight." The speech hinted at more courage than I actually felt.

After ordering the cadets back to their classes, Palomino walked me to the exit and gave me a firm hug. A profound sense of melancholy washed over me. I was turning away from the life I knew here. This goodbye meant there was no going back.

As the days, weeks, and months went by, my vision grew worse. Colors and shapes became progressively less distinct. The doctors said I had developed glaucoma, which caused excessive pressure within the eye. Glaucoma is a leading cause of blindness, and it was very likely I would lose the little bit of sight I managed to recover.

I almost didn't go to the graduation ceremony for my class on December 19. It seemed so unfair. I had come so close to realizing my dream of becoming a police detective. The very thought of not standing with my fellow classmates at this time of personal triumph and recognition now seemed agonizing. In the final analysis though, I knew I had to go. I would never be able to get on with my life unless I did.

The morning was clear, and the sun felt warm on my face.

Hundreds of excited family members could be heard talking all around me. I felt fortunate to be seated two rows behind the president, Alan García Pérez, who would present swords to each of the new lieutenants from the Guardia Civil and Guardia Republicana. President García Pérez would also present the Silver Insignia (the Peruvian equivalent of the FBI Shield) to the new detectives. The new lieutenants from Guardia Civil were called first, followed by the new detectives. The new lieutenants and detectives formed up according to their performance class rankings.

In my mind, I calculated where I would have been standing among my classmates and felt a sudden surge of conflicting emotions. I was happy for my classmates and their families, of course, but I was also devastated because I was not taking part. I could hear the precise footsteps as the new detectives approached the podium and the sharp crack of their heels as they stood at attention in front of the president. I would have given anything to be standing up there waiting to receive my Silver Insignia. A knot formed in my throat, and I felt close to tears. I was glad to be wearing dark glasses.

I thought back to my first day at the detective academy. The induction of my class had been inaugurated with a special ceremony before the general, other officers, and our family members. As the band played a military anthem, my heart swelled with pride at the thought of becoming a protector of society and the nation. Our families were very proud and happily applauded our acceptance into the detective academy. We knew that, after four years of rigorous training, we would become officers and would fight organized crime and terrorists. For me, that dream had evaporated. The image I had of myself as a valiant officer of peace had been dashed. Only a void remained now. Still, attending the graduation ceremony had been difficult, but necessary. I had to close that door behind me if I was ever going to plot a new course forward.

At the conclusion of the graduation ceremony, my class again fell into formation. One of the top two graduates, William Llanos, led us in the detective anthem. We then gathered in a hall where President García Pérez and Minister of Interior Abel Salina saluted the new officers with champagne.

I had the opportunity to shake hands with the president and ask about my pension and the possibility of going back to the US for more surgery. President García Pérez did not seem especially interested. He brushed me off quickly and impatiently referred me to the minister of interior, who was standing next to him. I shook Minister Salina's hand and repeated my request. He brusquely responded in a dismissive manner, telling me to make an appointment with the director of the National Police.

Their apparent lack of concern was extremely disheartening. I had served my country well with honor and distinction, at great personal sacrifice. These politicians, I realized, didn't care. They didn't truly value the members of the police force. I felt unwanted and very alone. I began to understand that, if I were going to have a future, it would have to be of my own making.

• Chapter Twelve •

CERCIL

Following the graduation ceremony, I had to decide what to do with the rest of my life. My vision was not getting any better, but I still had hope. I hoped additional medical options might still be considered. I was not ready to accept life as a blind man with one hand. I felt certain that such a life could not possibly hold any promise of success or happiness—so that was no kind of life for me.

The pain in my left eye was getting worse. It felt like I had sand in my eye that wouldn't wash out. In January, I went back to the Mogrovejo Hospital to see what could be done. A doctor told me my cornea had been damaged, and he thought an implant might improve my vision. I'll take any improvement, I thought. Even if all I could see were colors and shadows, it would be better than nothing at all. I wanted to believe that this was the way to go.

The eye doctor referred me to Dr. Contreras, a cornea specialist. I went to his office feeling good about the appointment. Dr. Contreras was very personable and interested in my case. I liked him right away. After reviewing the medical records, he told me about the rehabilitation services from Centro de Rehabilitacion de Ciegos de Lima (CERCIL), in English, the Rehabilitation Center for the Blind of Lima. He was a member of the board of directors and offered to write a letter of introduction. What he said sounded good. I assumed they would provide therapy to improve my vision.

Mama and I went to CERCIL the very next day. I really didn't know what to expect, but I tried to be positive. I was holding Mama's arm when she came to a shuddering stop just as we entered the building.

"Oh," she gasped. Her body trembled, and she started to sob.

"Mama, what's wrong?" I wanted to know. Her reaction really scared me.

"Oh, Carlos," she said softly so only I should hear. "Everyone here is blind. They all have white canes."

Mama knew, of course, that this was a center for the blind, but until she actually saw blind people for herself, she had nursed her own kind of denial. I had once been part of one of the most prestigious institutions in Peru, a young man with a bright future. Being here in this building forced her to confront the harsh reality. Her son was blind. Nothing would ever be the same again. She knew people would treat me differently now. Many will think me unable to make a good living or have a normal life. The sudden realization proved too much for her.

My own reaction was more reserved. I had come with the illusion that there might be some kind of therapy that might restore at least some of my sight. I began to suspect that this was not that kind of place. Still, I wanted to know more about what they actually did here.

A receptionist talked to Mama gently and helped her compose herself. Then she took us to meet Dr. Urcia, the director. We gave him Dr. Contreras's letter. Dr. Urcia was professional and welcoming. He described CERCIL's training and declared with conviction that, "It is respectable to be blind." That sounded good to me. He also said that CERCIL could teach me how to travel independently on my own using a white cane, read and write using Braille, and live on my own with the right training. I might even be able to do a little work to keep myself busy.

Since my injury, I had had to depend on others for almost everything. I felt totally out of control and helpless most of the time. I hated that. CERCIL did not offer the therapy I was hoping for, but it did offer a way for me to be more independent as I explored other options for the future. I didn't really believe that I would always be blind, but I had to learn how to take care of myself now. CERCIL was what I needed at this point in my life. I wanted to go places without being escorted everywhere. I didn't want people, family and friends especially, to be required to jump every time I made a move.

I told Dr. Urcia that I wanted to start right away. I felt good about my decision. I could feel some of my old self-determination coming back.

CERCIL was located on Avenida Pardo in Miraflores, in an old house donated by a middle-class family several years earlier. It had six rooms, a restroom for the employees, and a separate restroom facility for the blind students. It was located in the backyard behind the building, and it had running water.

The teachers and therapist were professional and skilled, and we could tell that they enjoyed their work. Mr. Livia had just one hand and was the only blind teacher. He taught me to use the slate and stylus (a portable frame for writing Braille). He also helped the students purchase collapsible white canes.

Patient and empathetic, he listened to our concerns, making him our favorite teacher and mentor.

We needed to learn to function efficiently and safely without sight. In the Daily Living Skills class, we learned how to cook, iron, clean, and engage in everyday activities as needed for independent living. Most of the students had grown up in very poor families, without electricity. They had to learn to use unfamiliar home appliances at the same time they were learning non-visual methods. The students who became blind as adults had to relearn how to live independently. The students who had been blind their whole lives started from scratch. A few weeks after I started my training, a new student started training, and I was surprised that it was Eduardo. He was the inmate who became blind when fighting while in prison.

Orientation and Mobility using a white cane was my favorite class. First, I learned how to hold and arc the cane as I found my way around the building. Then I was sent to explore the neighborhood, paying attention to environmental cues to maintain my orientation. Gradually, as I went further afield, I gained the confidence to travel into unfamiliar areas. Eventually, I was able to go anywhere I wanted in Lima using public transportation. Some areas had no sidewalks, and the streets were not always paved, which made them a challenge to navigate. On occasion, I bumped into or tripped over things in my way, encountered holes in the sidewalk, and ran into windows opened to the street. It was all part of the learning process, and I loved it. Knowing that I didn't have to wait for someone to take me places boosted my self-confidence tremendously. My mental health improved greatly, and the people close to me could tell the difference. I was taking charge of my life again. I was blind, but not defeated.

My girlfriend, Mary, and I, however, were not doing so well. This was not a casual relationship. We were a handsome couple, and I thought we had a strong relationship based on love and understanding. That all changed when I lost my right hand and became blind. When I felt most beaten down and close to despair, Mary was never there for me. She couldn't help me imagine a good life as a blind person. She simply did not believe such a thing was possible. She thought it was ludicrous to even think I could have a normal life with a career and family. I had my own doubts as well, of course, but I wanted to believe otherwise.

I didn't make it easy for Mary, either. I frequently lost my temper whenever I was frustrated with some situation caused by blindness. At such times, I often took it out on Mary. If Mama was around, I dumped my anger on her as well. Of course, Mama, being Mama, always forgave me and tolerated my bad behavior. Not Mary. She fought back.

When I told Mary how I thought college could prepare me for a rewarding career, she shot the idea down as completely unrealistic and foolish. "How do you think you could graduate from college?" she wanted to know. "Even if they let you graduate, who would hire you?"

"I could start my own business," I countered.

"You really think so?" she said. "You would never be able to keep track of your inventory. How would you manage your money? People would be taking advantage of you all the time. It could never work."

Our fights turned more cruel and became more frequent. We thought it might be good for us both if we broke up for a while. When we did, I experienced pain almost immediately. I didn't want to end things. I wanted Mary to understand me, to support me. I wanted her to tell me that I wasn't crazy to believe I could still have a normal life.

I was beside myself with misery. I went through hell, convinced we had made a mistake. Before long, I began searching her out, wanting to get back together again. When we did, it always ended the same way with more shouting and recriminations.

Mary lived with her parents just a few houses down from where I lived with my family. One night, my little brother Ernesto ran to tell me that he had just seen her going into her home. I went over to knock on the door with Ernesto tagging along.

"Who is it?" a voice came down from a second-story window.

I stepped back from the door and turned my face up so Mary's mother could see who it was.

"Hello, ma'am," I said. "Can I see Mary?"

"Mary's not home yet," Mrs. Ormeño said. "In fact, I don't expect to see her back anytime soon. She's doing some kind of research for school and might not get home until late tonight."

In the past, Mary's mother usually invited me in to sit for a while on those occasions when Mary wasn't there when I came looking for her. I couldn't remember her doing that since I became blind. When I didn't say anything right away, she repeated herself.

"She won't get home until late tonight, very late."

Ernesto and I didn't say anything to each other as we walked slowly back home. I had been humiliated. Ernesto knew full well that Mrs. Ormeño was lying. He had seen Mary just minutes before. That he should be witness to the shameful way I had been treated was embarrassing. More than that, I felt angry. After all, Mrs. Ormeño's behavior reflected the way her daughter regarded our relationship. Mary was avoiding me.

Then I heard she was dating someone else. I began to realize that it wasn't possible for Mary to be in a relationship with a blind man. She was incapable of giving me the emotional support I needed. Though hard to accept, I finally understood that our relationship had to end. When I accepted that, I never tried to see her again.

A few weeks later, I met Patricia, and we began seeing each other. Her mother, however, strenuously opposed our relationship—because I was blind, not studying, and not working. As far as she was concerned, I had no future. Patricia, to her credit, went against her mother's wishes and continued seeing me anyway.

Dating caused me no end of self-doubt and mental anguish. The thing was, a part of me understood Patricia's mother's point of view. She saw me as damaged goods, and I couldn't entirely disagree. How could I ask someone to give themselves to a relationship with me, a blind person? What did I have to offer, really? Could I support a wife and kids? Maybe Patricia's mother was right.

Given my inner turmoil, I was reluctant to commit myself fully to Patricia. I also didn't want to come between her and her mother. It quickly became apparent to both of us that it just wasn't working, so we stopped dating. That breakup impacted me deeply. I began to despair of ever being able to marry and have a family.

When people first meet, some of the most common questions are, "What do you do? Are you married? Do you have children?" So much of our self-identity and sense of community is tied to things like school, work, marriage, close relationships, or children. Truth was, I had little to connect me to others. I felt incomplete, not entirely credible, like an outsider always looking in but not participating in life. I had no sense of belonging and very little self-esteem.

I found inspiration in self-help books recorded on audio-cassette available through the small Talking Book Program for the Blind at CERCIL. This kind of reading reinforced the values I gained from my parents, teachers, and the other influential people in my life. According to Og Mandino, one of my favorite authors, we rise to achieve our full potential during times of greatest adversity and challenge. It is human nature to survive. Literature like this charged me with energy and determination. As Papa would have said, *"¡Esto no me va a vencer!"* ("This is not going to defeat me!")

A few weeks before finishing my training at CERCIL, I needed to cross a busy street when I heard a couple of young men talking. It sounded like they were planning a party.

"Hey, you guys. Can you help me cross the street?" I asked as I approached them, tapping my cane.

One of them broke out laughing loudly. The other guy laughed too, but not nearly so hard. Apparently, my inability to cross the street unassisted struck them as hilarious. I could feel my missing hand balling up into a fist.

"Hey dude, we are also blind!" the first guy said, still laughing. "What's your name? Are you from CERCIL? Where do you live?"

That is how I met Marcos. Coincidentally, he lived three blocks from my house in San Juan. We had attended the same high school. We quickly became good friends. He was positive, upbeat, and determined to live a full and active life. He was the first positive blind role model I met who was also close to me in age.

Marcos was about to graduate with his bachelor's degree in education. He had an older blind sister who was studying law and a younger blind brother who was a senior in high school. They all had positive attitudes, and they were entirely comfortable with their blindness. Marcos and his siblings were exactly the kind of blind people I needed to associate with. They helped me understand that blind people could be productive and have normal lives. It felt empowering to realize I was not deluding myself. If they could think of themselves as no different from sighted people, I could think of myself that way, too.

I thought back to the friends I had before I became blind.

My school, neighborhood, and detective academy friends were motivated, positive, and optimistic, inspiring me to be like them. Now that I was blind, I needed encouragement and motivation more than ever. Blind friends like Marcos helped me realize that I could have a good life and be happy. I wanted to be like Marcos.

Chapter Thirteen

CATI

After graduating from CERCIL, I looked for ways to support myself. My friend Marcos helped me tremendously. He was earning extra money selling quality imported items picked up from Tacna and sold again for a profit in Lima. He encouraged me to give that a try, and so I did.

Tacna is near the Chilean border, a twenty-four-hour bus ride from Lima. I bought fabric for dresses and suits, wrist-watches, perfumes, novelty items for the home, jewelry, and makeup. The plan was to bring back small items that could be sold quickly. As I got to know other blind people, they gave me tips on how to judge the quality of items for purchase and resale. They also told me how to handle my money and protect myself from others who would take advantage of me.

I never had to travel very far by bus before, and I found the ride to Tacna to be tiring, uncomfortable, and boring.

Sitting for such a long time in the same position and trying to sleep was miserable. When we stopped for meals, we took advantage of the opportunity to walk around, get some fresh air, and look for restrooms. Sometimes we came to police checkpoints. The police would stop the bus to examine documents and check for terrorists wanted by the Peruvian minister of justice.

One particular bus ride to Tacna stands out. Marcos sat in front of my brother Enrique and me. Enrique sat by the window watching the scenery, which he occasionally described to me, and I sat on the aisle. Across from me sat a small child, around eight years old, accompanied by his father. After a while, Marcos, Enrique, and I ran out of things to talk about, so I began talking to my young neighbor, who apparently had been closely observing us for several hours.

With the curiosity typical of children, the boy asked, "Why do you use that cane?"

Candid questions like this didn't bother me. In fact, I was happy to answer the boy. I told him I was blind and that my cane helped me get around when there was no one to guide me. I wanted him to feel comfortable asking questions.

"Do you see anything at all?"

"No."

Then the boy's father broke into the conversation, insisting that I wasn't being truthful. I was just messing with his son's head, he said.

"Look carefully. He has only one eye," the father pointed out, "kind of cloudy, but the other one looks fine. Also, he looks at you when you're talking."

The boy came right back at me. "How come your right eye looks normal, and you're looking at me?"

Realizing that the boy's father thought I was faking my blindness, I smiled and continued.

"I can hear where your voice is coming from, so that's

where I look. My right eye looks normal because it is a prosthetic eye."

"What is a prosthetic eye?"

"It is an artificial eye, made of a type of plastic called acrylic."

The boy turned back to his father. "What about that, Papa?"

"Don't believe him. He's pulling your leg. He's not really blind."

The boy was indignant. "Papa says you're not blind."

Other conversations around us stopped as people started listening to us. Smiling at the boy, I reached up to tap my prosthetic eye with a fingernail, making a tapping sound.

"See, Papa, his eye is fake!" the boy said excitedly.

The father was not convinced. "No," he assured his son, "he was pretending. That was his teeth you heard." He clicked his own teeth to make the point. I wasn't sure, but I thought he probably pretended to tap his eye at the same time he clicked his teeth.

The boy was confused. "You're making that noise with your teeth," he said, not knowing who to believe.

By now, we had a captive audience. Still smiling, I took a tissue from my pocket and told my new friend to look at my right eye.

"Look carefully at my right eye." Using the tissue, I slowly took out the eye and opened my eyelids wide so that the boy could see the empty socket.

"WOW! Papa, do you see that? Can you do it?" exclaimed the excited boy. I knew without a doubt the boy now believed me.

The father said nothing more, but I knew he was listening.

Having proved I was blind, I went on to tell him about blindness. I told him about how I read using a system of raised dots called Braille and how a slate and stylus are used to write

Braille. I shared with him how blind people live on their own using non-visual ways of doing things, and I told him about my trip to Tacna.

I was happy to help educate the little boy but troubled to think that some sighted people would assume I was faking blindness.

I only traveled to Tacna four times. I made very little money. The time on the bus and the cost of buying food along the way made the venture not worth my time.

One day I stopped by CERCIL in hopes of selling my few remaining items. I stood in the doorway of the Daily Living Skills class clicking my heels together, a habit from my days as a cadet at the detective academy.

"Deborah?" I asked, standing erect, awaiting a response from the teacher.

"No," a pleasant voice answered. She sounded friendly.

"Miriam?" I asked again, thinking that it might be the occupational therapist.

"No," she answered warmly, sounding amused.

I gave up. "I'm sorry. Who are you, and what are you doing here?"

"I teach here. So, who are you, and what are you doing here?" she came right back at me, clearly enjoying herself, this time with a little laugh.

I smiled and told her my name, but I did not offer her my items from Tacna, because I did not know her. I told her I was a CERCIL graduate and asked for her name.

"My name is Cati, and I started working here last week."

I liked her name, her voice, and the chance way we had met. I visited CERCIL more frequently, and soon Cati and I became friends. I waited for her to finish work at 1:00 most afternoons. We would go to lunch and, afterward, I accompanied her to the bus stop. I felt at ease and happy to be with her. Unlike many other people, she was comfortable with my blindness. To Cati, blindness was entirely normal.

Cati had just graduated from the School of Medicine from the San Marcos National University, and she relished the opportunity to tell me all about the field of occupational therapy. One afternoon, after finishing our lunch, we strolled the streets of Miraflores, and I mentioned that I hadn't been to a movie in more than a year. She said we should go together, and she would describe the movie. It was September. A few days later, Cati and I went to watch *The Secret of My Success*. We were officially a couple.

Cati and I had similar backgrounds. Her father was a retired police officer—very strict—and the kind of man who commands immediate respect. Both of our families valued discipline, hard work, and respect for others. Our families had similar incomes, similar standards of living, and very similar values. We got along well. Even though we were two young people who had chosen very different careers, we had much in common. As we got to know each other better and better, we enjoyed viewing the world from each other's perspectives.

With the CERCIL training as a foundation, it was time to get on with life. I wanted to start school. Cati had taken classes at the English Institute and had her teaching certificate. She encouraged me to study English. Even though I did not like it in high school, I enrolled in an English class. Since it was only one two-hour class per day, it gave me time to find readers, transcribe my lessons into Braille, and study. Cati and two friends from my neighborhood read to me while I made Braille notes. Then they recorded the lessons on a tape so I could practice my English pronunciation.

I was cautious not to enter a new relationship too quickly, afraid to invest myself emotionally. I did not want to be hurt again. My reticence, as it turned out, gave us time to develop a strong relationship slowly. I learned to trust her implicitly as we grew closer together.

Just like my relationship with Patricia, I was afraid Cati's parents would object to me as a blind man dating their daughter. I was right. Her father made it clear that he did not approve and prohibited Cati from seeing me. Cati could not understand her father's attitude, but I could.

As a brother with four sisters, I would not want them to marry someone who could not provide for them. I would not want my widowed mother to marry an unproductive person. If I had a daughter, I would not want her to date or marry someone who had no future. I truly understood her father's feelings. He must have seen me as unlikely to provide for his daughter in any meaningful way.

Mary's and Patricia's parents, I'm sure, had the same reservations, and that played a large part in those relationships ending. Knowing that, I was never angry with Cati's father. Instead, I viewed the situation objectively and maturely. I was blind, and it was natural for Cati's family to have doubts. While emotionally difficult, I knew I had to face the situation with a positive attitude. I would not force Cati to choose between her father and me. I did not use Cati's disappointment in her father's decision to manipulate her feelings. On the contrary, I told her it was natural for her father to want to protect her and to assume that her feelings for me came from a place of kindness and pity. I understood his feelings. At the same time, I was determined to show that I could be productive and successful. I still hoped I would get my vision back. In the meantime, I would not be idle or passive. I would look for opportunities. To be successful, I knew I had to develop a clear and strong sense of purpose.

• Chapter Fourteen •

LA UNIVERSIDAD

Cati and I spent more and more time together as the attraction we felt for each other grew stronger. The world just felt like a better place when Cati and I were together. I never thought my blindness made any difference to her. It got to be very easy for me to open up and trust her with my hopes and fears for the future.

One warm summer afternoon, we were walking along the median strip of Pardo Avenue toward Kennedy Park when I brought up the idea of college. "You know," I started tentatively, "I think I might want to go back to school and learn how to do something." I hoped she wouldn't think that I was crazy or try to dissuade me.

"Oh," she said slowly, "you don't sound too sure about that."

"Well, actually, I was thinking about studying law, but I

would have to take the admissions test first."

"Okay," she said, sounding interested. "Where would you go?"

"San Martin University," I said without conviction.

"When are you planning to take the test?"

"Whenever the next test is scheduled," I said, hoping to sound more confident than I felt. I didn't ask her what she thought about me attending classes at San Martin, for fear of what she might say.

The conversation turned in other directions as we continued our walk. It occurred to me that she probably didn't want to hurt my feelings and thought it kinder to just drop the subject.

A week later, we were once again walking on the avenue enjoying another warm summer day, when she announced, "I have the admission package and the application form for the next entrance exam for San Martin. Do you want me to read it to you?"

My heart leaped with joy. Cati believed in me after all. She didn't doubt that I could be successful.

The people who were close to me before I became blind and knew me best, my family and friends, supported me, too, in their way, but it was not the same. Mama, especially, did not ever try to discourage me from doing whatever I wanted, but she worried for me. She didn't want to see me hurt.

My friends and other family members also tried to help me in whatever small ways they could, but, when it came right down to it, they didn't believe that I could actually have a good life—and be independent. They did not really believe in blind people. I imagined them feeling sorry for me. Blindness had diminished my prospects for the future in their eyes. Any chance I had of accomplishing anything significant in life was most unlikely. For all I knew, they might be right.

Cati was different. We had been growing gradually closer

together for some time, but when she finally made it clear to me that she would stand by me, wherever our dreams for each other took us, I gave myself completely to her. My heart and mind were in total agreement. Cati was the person I wanted to be my partner in life. It was a new and deeper love than I had ever known before.

I asked her to please read the admissions information. Confident that I had her support now, I felt motivated and energized to get going. I wanted with all my heart to start a new and productive life.

I applied for entrance to San Martin the next day. Once again, I found myself preparing for another admissions test to a prestigious institution, but this time I was blind. Still, my previous experience gave me an advantage. I knew how to prepare for an entrance examination. Drawing on my self-discipline, determination, and the techniques learned from other blind people, I got ready. Over the next several weeks, friends read to me to help me prepare for the rigorous test.

On the day of the examination, I was extremely nervous. I hadn't slept well the night before. I worried that my mind would wander and I would make mistakes. I was afraid the accommodations the university made for me as a blind applicant would be inadequate. Would I be able to finish the test in the allotted time? So much could go wrong.

At the law school on Javier Prado Avenue, I joined a large group of young people waiting to take the admissions test. The tenseness in the air from the students as we waited felt familiar.

We entered, and I was led to a separate room where a reader waited. As she began reading the test questions, I still felt nervous, but I quickly relaxed as we went along. When I didn't know an answer to a question, I told her to skip it. We would come back to it later, I said, if there was time at the end. She did everything I wanted with no problems. I finished the examination with time to spare. I thought I had done alright, but I would have to wait for the test results to be posted next week. It didn't quite happen that way.

Before the test scores could be released, a legal dispute disrupted the university administration. Two people claimed to be the university's legitimate president, and the examination results would not be released until the issue had been resolved.

I was lying in bed enjoying the sun and cool air coming in through the bedroom window one morning around 7:00 several weeks later, listening to the news on television. Suddenly, my immediate and full attention came into sharp focus. The San Martin University dispute had been resolved, the announcer said. Alberto Fujimori, chair of the National Council of University Presidents, had successfully mediated the problem. The law school examination results were in the morning papers.

I got up, turned off the television, and called my best friend, Juan Jimenez. Juan and I had known each other since we had been small children in the neighborhood. Half asleep, Juan answered the phone. I asked him to go out with me to pick up a newspaper. After hearing the news, he immediately agreed. In less than two minutes, we were on our way.

We walked three blocks in anticipatory silence to the northwest corner of Tomás Guzmán y Joaquin Bernal streets to buy the paper from a street vendor. Juan quickly scanned it for the list of applicants accepted for law school, but he couldn't find it. We asked the woman selling newspapers if there was more to the paper. Without speaking, she brought out another section from under the counter. (At that time, in Lima, newspaper sellers frequently held back important sections of the paper to make extra money.)

As we walked back along Tomás Guzmán Avenue with my left hand on Juan's right shoulder, he searched the paper for the names of people who passed the admissions examination to the law school. Half a block away from the newspaper stand, he found the list. Slowing down to read while avoiding holes in the street, Juan didn't see my name. I tensed with anticipation as I waited.

"Carlos, your name isn't here," Juan said finally. "Do they list the first or last name first?" he asked, not really sounding very hopeful.

I didn't say anything. Though the morning was warm and clear, I felt cold inside. The disappointment was crushing. We walked in complete silence, my shoulders slouched. I felt totally dejected. I listened to our footsteps on the pavement, the sound of passing cars, and the rustling of the newspaper brushing against Juan's left leg as we walked.

My heart and my will felt empty, devastated. I had worked so hard to get ready for this test. If I couldn't get into law school, what was I to do? I was overcome with despair. The only other time I felt this way was when I failed to be accepted into officers school. I had been turned away, the door slammed in my face. I might never have an opportunity like this again.

Lost in thought, I considered the possibility that Juan made a mistake. Did he really examine the list carefully? He might have read just the first half of the list and missed the names beginning with *S*. I was grasping at straws, and I knew it.

"Hey Juan, did you look for my last name under *S*?" I asked hesitantly. It was a stupid question. People often made the mistake of spelling my name with a *C*, but Juan knew how to spell my name.

We were now in the street in front of the school for students with special needs, Our Lady of Guadalupe, a block away from my house. For a few seconds, Juan didn't say anything. Then he came to an abrupt stop and exclaimed, "Oh shit! Serván is spelled with an *S*, of course! I'm an idiot!"

Juan quickly reopened the newspaper and hurriedly rifled

through the pages. I waited, afraid of being disappointed again.

Then, after some of the longest seconds of my life, he spoke again. "Here you are! Serván Triveño, Carlos Rigoberto. They even got the Rigoberto! Holy shit, Carlos, this is you! There's no other Carlos Rigoberto! Congratulations, dude!"

My best friend from the *barrio* was the first to congratulate me and give me a hug. With my spirits restored, my shoulders straightened, we rushed back home. I felt exhilarated but also uncertain. I needed to find the money for tuition. I also needed to commit myself to my studies, this time as a blind student. How was I going to manage the challenges I was sure to face?

Hoping for good news, my mother and sister Vicky were hovering near the front door, waiting for our return. Juan told me later they looked fearful at first when we walked in, but they both broke into wide smiles when they saw how happy we were.

"I heard you calling Juan about the test results, and knew that you went to find out if you passed." Vicky gave me a big hug.

Mama was also very happy for me, but also a little miffed. "Why didn't you tell me you had applied to study law?" she scolded gently.

I reminded her that it had always been my way to wait until I had good news to share. Mama made it clear that she would always support me, no matter what. Juan gave me one more congratulatory hug before going home.

Then I rushed to my room upstairs to call Cati and tell her the wonderful news. "Guess what?"

"You got accepted!" she said, smiling.

"How did you know?"

"I heard on the news the results had been released."

"Yeah, but how did you know that I had been accepted?" I persisted.

"You have been studying hard, and I've been watching you. I know when someone is well prepared for an exam. You prepared well. Don't tell me you had doubts!"

I told her that no one could be entirely sure until the results have been released, but I knew I had the ability to pass the entrance examination. Had it not been the case, I never would have tried.

Cati's confidence in me—and my ability to function as a blind person—was truly marvelous. The more I got to know Cati, the more convinced I was of our compatibility and love.

An old saying came to mind, "Tell me who your friends are, and I will tell you who you are." That doesn't just apply to friendships; it also applied to the person you choose to spend the rest of your life with.

It had been a good day. That afternoon and evening, visitors flooded the house. One after another, my friends came to congratulate me, as Juan was quick to spread the good news far and wide. I had been accepted into the university! It was time to celebrate.

A few months later, Cati accepted my proposal of marriage. We were engaged, but we wouldn't actually marry until I had a stable job and the means to support us. Cati's father still thought of me as inappropriate for his eldest daughter. I had to prove to him, her family, and to myself that I could provide for her and our eventual family. I also had to prove Cati wanted to be with me, not out of pity, but out of love. It was essential that her family trust me and believe that I had no intention of being a burden to Cati.

A week before classes started, Cati and I were walking the streets of Miraflores again when I told her that I was going to need some kind of part-time job. For once, Cati disagreed.

"I don't think so. You are going to need all the time outside classes you can manage to read the assignments, do research, and write papers. You won't have time to work," Cati explained patiently. "Law school classes will be very different from those at the detective academy. Your professors will demand so much of you."

"How is that going to work? I won't be able to support myself or pay tuition? How will I buy food?" I wanted to know. We headed toward the bus stop where Cati would catch the bus home.

"I can help with your expenses."

Cati's matter-of-fact pronouncement caught me by surprise. I couldn't say anything for a long moment, thinking about what she just said. I wasn't angry. My feelings weren't hurt. My pride wasn't wounded. Rather, I was deeply moved. Cati believed in me, loved me, and would stand by me. I would not ask her to pay for my tuition or other expenses, but her love and confidence in me felt wonderful and made me unimaginably happy. I didn't know what to say, overwhelmed with love for her. The only way I could respond was to hug her closer as we walked.

My mind shifted back to the practicalities of law school. I needed to find a way to read my assignments. My strategy was pretty simple: Make friends with the more studious types in my classes, and then ask them to read for me. But finding them proved to be more difficult than I anticipated. I discovered that many students skipped classes and just wanted to party. Others just wanted to find a boyfriend or girlfriend. Many students' attitudes were very different from the attitudes of the cadets at the detective academy.

Eventually, I got three of my classmates to read for me. It was a win-win relationship. They liked reading for me because it forced them to read the assignments out loud, which helped them remember the material and retain it better. I appreciated their help, but I needed more readers. My three friends weren't enough to get me through all of my assignments.

I took advantage of every opportunity to recruit readers.

When I ran into friends at the bus stop or on the bus, I asked them to read a few pages. They seemed happy to read for me, and their encouragement motivated me to study hard and keep pushing toward my goals. I did not want to impose, but law school was demanding. I had to find more readers. I was always looking for help, and people seldom rejected my appeals. Even so, it never seemed to be enough. I constantly worried about falling behind.

I went to visit a friend from the detective academy one evening, Juan Usin Vasquez. He had been two classes ahead of me and became paraplegic just a few weeks before graduation. He was unemployed at the time. We shared the disappointment of having our dreams of becoming detectives cut short. After reminiscing about old times, I told him I was studying law at the University of San Martin. He was excited and offered to read for me.

Juan took his role seriously. We worked together for hours each day, and he quizzed me to see how well I knew the material. After several months of hard work, it was time for final examinations. I took all of my finals orally, and scored above average in all my classes, earning my two highest grades in the classes Juan helped with. He was almost as happy as I was. We celebrated our accomplishment with crackers and Inca Cola.

Chapter Fifteen

THE LORD OF MIRACLES

Every October in Lima, hundreds of thousands of people fill the streets for El Señor de los Milagros, the Procession of Our Lord of Miracles, one of Peru's oldest Catholic celebrations. This sacred event, also known as Christ of Miracles, is named for a mural of Jesus Christ painted in 1651 by an African slave. When earthquakes destroyed most of Lima, the holy mural was miraculously spared.

A brotherhood of select members of the church carries a large, elaborate, ornate wooden frame containing a replica of the mural through the streets of Lima. The Procession of Our Lord of Miracles is one of the largest religious events in the world, drawing hundreds of thousands of believers. The president of Peru, the mayor of Lima, and the archbishop of Lima all participate in the event. The procession circles downtown Lima and takes twenty hours to complete. For some reason, I felt compelled to attend this crowded celebration.

The idea of participating in such a large and important event on my own overwhelmed me, but I needed to confront my fears and uncertainty. And in 1988, I felt called, compelled, to get as close to the famous mural replica of Jesus as I could.

During the Procession of Our Lord of Miracles, the brotherhood uses a thick long rope to make a 40-by-80-foot rectangular fence around the painting of Jesus Christ. The fence allows them to move through the crowd of people and protect the painting.

I set out alone. My goal was to touch the rope fence. When I arrived at the main downtown bus stop, I had no idea how I would make my way through the crowd or how I would find the rope. I took out my white cane, unfolded it, and walked toward the procession. After several blocks, I reached Colon Road and, soon after, Alfonso Ugarte Avenue, just as the procession advanced toward Plaza Dos de Mayo. I focused on reaching the rope and kept walking. From a distance, I could hear the band and choir that walk right behind the painting of Christ. Crowds filled the streets, which had been blocked off from regular traffic. I followed the wave of religious supplicants. The sweet smell of Peruvian desserts like mazamorra morada, picarones, and turrones filled the air. I made my way ever closer to the sound of the band.

I just needed to follow the advancing multitude. The more crowded it got, the closer I got to my goal. As I neared the roped-off processional, I maneuvered between people, pushing and being pushed. It became impossible to use my cane in the dense crowd, so I folded it and tied it to my belt. The scent of incense grew stronger. I knew I was close. My dream? To reach the rope and accompany the painting of Christ for an hour. I repeated to myself, "A little closer. A little closer. A bit more, and you will get there, Carlos." Being at least a head taller than most people, six feet tall and 190 pounds helped me work my way through the crowd—or maybe my size convinced people to allow me through. Finally, I reached the rope!

Pleased, I walked slowly, holding onto the rope, accompanying the procession. I felt the energy and excitement of the hundreds of thousands of believers who walked through the streets. The members of the brotherhood walked inside the rope rectangle carrying the painting of Christ. Every few yards, members of the brotherhood stopped, still holding the rope, to make certain that no one trespassed the barrier. They acted like police—tough, inflexible, and resolute. A few minutes later, I heard a brotherhood member call, "Serván." The voice came from somewhere within the roped-off area. I turned my head toward the sound and heard my name called again. A moment later, someone touched my left arm.

Confused and still walking slowly with the crowd, I asked, "Who are you?"

"This is Cabezas. Are you by yourself?" Cabezas graduated from the detective school in the class two years ahead of mine. Still holding my arm, he said, "Come in! Go under the rope!" Inside the rope, I felt safer, no longer pushed by the crowd. I gave my friend a warm hug.

As we walked, I heard a strong, authoritative voice boom, "The order is to let no one inside the rope. Why are you letting him in?" I felt Cabezas gesture with his hands, letting the other man know that I was blind, and he stopped yelling.

The voice belonged to the head of the brotherhood. He came over to me, gave me a strong hug, and said, "Come with me, brother." After a few steps, he ordered the procession to stop. I could not believe it; they were stopping the procession for me! The men carrying the painting stopped, and he counted to three. Then a bell sounded. The carriers lowered the huge frame. It had a very heavy wood base with several wooden legs as thick as two human legs. It was five feet tall and so heavy it needed forty men to bear its weight. The men used special techniques to raise the painting, to advance, to stop, and to lower it down.

The head of the brotherhood asked me to come closer to it. The frame had a wooden ladder. In a kind voice, he told me to touch the ladder and start climbing. As I climbed, I passed roses and other flowers, their scent thick and sweet. The head of the brotherhood guided my hand toward the heart-quickening, sacred painting, and, when I touched it, goose bumps rose on my arms. Truly, I felt the presence of God in my soul.

In that sacred moment, I did not ask God why He allowed me to become blind. I did not ask for my eyesight back. I felt God speak to me, telling me He had other plans for my life. It was an epiphany—an indescribably strong emotional moment. As I spoke silently to God, I felt tremendous energy. I told God I did not question my blindness and the loss of my hand. I asked only for the strength, wisdom, and determination to face the obstacles before me and help to overcome them. I asked Him to show me the way to my new life. I felt God's presence envelop me like a hug, and a tender warmth spread throughout my body. I knew at that moment that God would never leave me. I felt unstoppable.

My attitude and life changed forever in that moment. I felt like the blind man in the Bible, Bartimaeus, who called out to Jesus from the roadside. Jesus, surrounded by a crowd, stopped and invited him to approach. With a touch, Christ healed Bartimaeus. While my physical blindness remains, my encounter with the Christ of Miracles healed my soul, and I received a clear vision of my future, a promise of hope, and an unshakable assurance of God's presence.

I don't remember how I left the procession, but do remember very clearly having a renewed energy and hope. I felt unstoppable.

That very day, I decided to move to the United States. I knew Peru offered only limited training and job opportunities for the blind. When I asked blind people in Peru what kind of work they did, they mentioned things like phone operator, massage therapist, musician, and teacher. I did not have musical talent. I did not have the patience to be a teacher. And I would have been bored working as a phone operator or massage therapist (not to mention hindered because I had only one hand). Some blind people studied law, as I did, but none actually practiced it.

I applied to the Ministry of Interior and the police for help getting to the United States. I hoped my younger brother, Enrique, who would soon turn nineteen, would be able to go with me. The long, complicated process required filling out countless documents, only to have them returned because of a missing comma or period. I talked to lawyers from the hospital, the police, and the Ministry of Interior. I collected signatures but had to return several times because the person whose signature I needed wasn't included. I needed signatures from the director of the hospital, the director of the police, and the minister of interior. Then I had to wait for the budget office to approve the funds. Fortunately, I got Enrique named in the resolution so he could travel with me and assist me in the United States.

While I completed the paperwork, William Llanos, a friend from the detective school, volunteered to raise money to help me make the move. He organized a large bingo event. The money would help with room and board as Enrique and I settled in. The kindness and generosity of my friends who coordinated, publicized, and ran the event touched my heart. I went to the fundraiser and stood by the door, welcoming and thanking people as they arrived. Former classmates from the detective school—people I hadn't seen in nearly three years—showed up, greeting me enthusiastically. Their support touched me deeply.

When I'd been hospitalized right after the accident, many of my classmates had visited me. Later, several bought my products from Tacna. I appreciated their friendship, but I could not rely on their help forever. I needed to be independent and productive. How exactly I would achieve that, remained elusive. But I had faith.

Once the various entities approved our documents, Enrique and I went to the American consulate in Miraflores to apply for his visa. (I had already received a medical visa.) We eagerly anticipated immigrating to the United States.

Speaking through a thick glass window, the American consul asked, "Do you have a college degree?"

"No," Enrique answered.

"Are you in college now?"

"No."

"Do you have a stable job?"

Enrique answered, "No." I could hear the worry in his voice.

"Do you speak English?"

Uneasy, Enrique answered softly, "No."

The interview ended abruptly. The American consul stamped Enrique's passport and said, "Visa denied."

Panicked, I asked, "Who will go with me? I cannot travel by myself."

Dispassionately, the American consul said, "The same person you traveled with last time—your mother."

This setback, though disappointing, would not stop me from moving to the United States. My mother would travel with me, leaving my little brother and sister, Ernesto and Gloria, at home. I had mixed feelings—excitement about immigrating to a new country coupled with sadness about leaving the country of my birth. I would miss my friends, family, and especially Cati. But I was determined to move to America for a better future, though unknown.

• Chapter Sixteen •

AMBITIOUS GOALS

As we walked the cold Baltimore streets in March 1989, Mama described piles of snow against the buildings. Curious, I reached down to touch the cold, wet stuff—something I'd never done in Lima, where the temperature never dropped below fifty-seven degrees. Every experience in America felt new, wondrous. I had come for a follow-up surgery at Johns Hopkins, but I had dreams of much more than that. I had a strong feeling that somehow I would find help in America.

The day after we arrived, Mama and I contacted José Alonso, a brother of a former classmate of Cati's. He and his wife came right over to meet us. From the start, I told them I intended to live in America. I'm sure they wondered what I thought a blind guy—who knew almost no English and had no work visa—could do in this country, or how they could help. Actually, they did a lot, especially providing us with transportation and helping us connect with needed resources. We quickly became very good friends.

First, I had to contact the medical staff at Johns Hopkins Hospital regarding follow-up surgery. After that, Mama and I needed to find more permanent accommodations than our hotel.

After two nights at the Sheraton, a friend of José's agreed to rent the living room space of his third-floor apartment on East Pratt Street to Mama and me. It wasn't ideal, but it would have to do until something better came along.

I had no problems with the admission to Johns Hopkins Hospital. All the endless forms I'd filled out in Peru cleared the way. The Ministry of Interior of Peru had completed the necessary paperwork for my surgery to take place in early April.

The day after the surgery, a nurse wheeled me into the doctor's office. After a brief examination, he paused, then spoke. "Unfortunately, the cornea transplant was unsuccessful. There is nothing more we can do."

I knew the prospects for a positive outcome from surgery had not been especially good and felt prepared for the bad news, but Mama wasn't. As we stood in the lobby after the meeting with the doctor, Mama started to cry and could not stop. The depth of her despair and grief startled me. I had never shared with her my own low expectations, but her reaction still surprised me. Though her sorrow broke my heart, my faith remained strong. I knew that I had been spared from death for a purpose. For some reason, I believed with all my heart that we would find an answer. The question was when and how, though.

We didn't have to wait long. As we stood in the lobby outside the doctor's office, Mama in tears, a man approached. "*Puedo ayudar?*" ("Can I help?") he asked.

I was so focused on trying to comfort Mama that I didn't even question this unlikely turn of events. In a hospital in

Baltimore, we happened to meet a man who speaks Spanish? Who offers to help?

In a strong Spanish accent, he told us he was from Texas. Mama struggled to control her sobs while she told him what had happened.

"Actually, I want to live in America, learn English, and eventually get a job," I interjected, not sure why I thought this man could do anything about our situation.

He assured us that we had done well to come to America. He believed we would find help here. He asked us to wait for a few minutes while he placed a call at a nearby pay phone. Several minutes later, he came back and gave us the number of a local church, the Spanish Apostolate, that we could contact for help.

"Good luck, young man!" He grabbed my left hand and shook it enthusiastically. "And don't give up!"

The next day, José took us to the Spanish Apostolate to learn about resources or services we could take advantage of. The Spanish Apostolate, a program of Catholic Charities of Baltimore, offered English as a Second Language (ESL) classes, a health clinic, legal services, and general assistance to immigrants. Finding this community, which allowed me to establish connections with the local Hispanic population, boosted my success. They had plenty of experience helping immigrants find work and adjust to living in a country with a new language, culture, and customs.

Sister Mary, the Spanish Apostolate director, met with us. In good but accented Spanish, she asked, "How can we help you?"

"I would like to go to college and work," I replied.

After a pause, Sister Mary said, with exasperation, "Well, you certainly don't ask for anything simple. What makes you think we can help you achieve such ambitious goals?"

I didn't know what to say. I had answered her question as

honestly and as sincerely as I could. So I didn't understand her irritation. I kept talking—in an effort to convince her I could succeed, but I just needed help.

Though Sister Mary understood my distress, she seemed unsure about how the Spanish Apostolate could help me achieve my goals, other than teaching me to speak English.

Back then, people couldn't just Google the solution to every problem. Not knowing what else to do, Sister Mary asked a staff person to look in the phone book for a place that helped blind people. And that's how I learned about the National Federation of the Blind (NFB).

The next day, a volunteer from the Spanish Apostolate drove Mama and me to the NFB's national headquarters. On the way, I thought about how to present myself. If necessary, I would act miserable and in need of charity. When she saw the NFB headquarters, Mama could not contain her amazement. She described a building several stories tall, filling an entire city block. I was impressed.

We took the elevator to the reception desk on the fourth floor. I thought, "Maybe the first three floors have dormitories where blind people live." I hoped the NFB would offer me a room and some meals. My mind raced with the possibilities.

Mama and I approached the reception desk as I held onto her arm. A young woman welcomed us. Quietly, Mama told me that the NFB building was very, very clean. The receptionist did not speak Spanish, so the Apostolate volunteer explained why we had come. While they talked, I did my best to look distressed and needy.

"I can't believe it!" Mama whispered to me. "She is blind! Her computer talks to her. She just took off the earphones connected to her computer and got her cane."

I was both impressed and surprised. I never knew a blind person could operate a computer and do so with such confidence and skill. The volunteer said that the receptionist left to find someone who spoke Spanish.

Mrs. Patricia Maurer came out to greet us. Dr. Marc Maurer was the president of the NFB, and Mrs. Maurer served as a full-time volunteer. Mrs. Maurer said she would call one of their Spanish-speaking members to talk directly with me and discuss what help the NFB could provide. Her response surprised me. Most people, whether they knew Spanish or not, typically spoke to the people with me, rather than to me, as if I were a child or not responsible for myself.

Mrs. Maurer called the Spanish-speaking member and explained the situation. Then she handed me the phone.

"My name is Eileen Rivera, and I am from Puerto Rico," a warm and friendly voice introduced herself in Spanish. "We would like to help you. But first, we need to know some more about you. My understanding is that you don't speak English. Right?"

"Right," I replied in Spanish.

"How old are you? What is your background? Do you read Braille and use a cane?"

I began to relax as I provided the information she wanted, but then she asked a question that perplexed me.

"What is your philosophy about blindness?"

Philosophy? What does philosophy have to do with anything? I thought. I didn't know where I could live or how I would feed myself. Who cares about philosophy? I realized, of course, that I should not say that just then. So, after giving it a minute's thought, I plunged ahead to answer her question. The words came from some place deep in my heart—the place where my dreams lived.

"I think that blind people can be independent when we get training and a chance to work," I said finally.

Eileen seemed delighted. "That's great! That's our philosophy too!"

Though I was glad Eileen liked my answer, I was a bit

confused. I had not come to the United States to be a philosopher. What was up with all this philosophy talk, anyway?

"What do you want to do in America?" Eileen continued kindly.

Well, after saying I believed in the ability of blind people to be self-supporting and independent, I could hardly say that I wanted to live rent-free in their building and be taken care of. I said, "I would like to go to college in America and, if possible, work to support myself."

Unlike Sister Mary, she seemed completely satisfied—comfortable even—with that answer. My ambitious goals didn't seem to faze Eileen. This made me curious about her.

"What do you do?" I asked her.

"I work at Johns Hopkins Hospital Wilmer Eye Institute," she said.

I imagined a nice, modern hospital, but assumed the work was similar to the work blind people did in Peru, perhaps packing medication into boxes. In Peru, blind people are given tedious, repetitive, low-skilled work, because it is assumed that they are good with their hands but incapable of doing much of anything else. At that time, they earned way less than minimum wage. In America, this would have been called sheltered employment for people with disabilities.

Eileen said that the NFB would do what they could to help. I gave her my address and phone number, but I didn't get my hopes up. Eileen sounded encouraging, but I had heard promises of assistance before, only to be disappointed.

After ending my call with Eileen, Mrs. Maurer gave me a long white cane that came up to the tip of my nose. The cane I had been using only came up to the bottom of my breastbone. She also gave me a couple of cassette tapes that had information in Spanish.

As we left the building, my shoulders sagged. I had come to the richest, most technologically advanced country in the world, and all I got was a long, white fiberglass cane and two cassette tapes—without even a tape recorder to play them on. I felt totally dejected.

I said little on the way back to the apartment. Then Mama told me something she hadn't mentioned before. Mrs. Maurer was also blind and carried a long white cane. That made a powerful impression on me. Just like the receptionist, Mrs. Maurer radiated confidence, something few blind people in Peru possessed.

Back at the apartment, I borrowed a tape recorder and listened to the tapes. They contained several articles by Dr. Kenneth Jernigan, the former president of the NFB. Thankfully, they'd been translated into Spanish. His words spoke to me as one blind person to another. He said that the blind needed to master the skills of blindness (also called alternative techniques). But he stated that the real problem blind people face is overcoming public misconceptions about the blind both from the blind and the sighted. With proper training and opportunity, the blind can be fully contributing members of society.

His message was exactly what I needed to hear. It energized me and filled me with a new sense of purpose and resolve to accomplish things I would not have thought possible just a few days earlier. What a divine coincidence that NFB headquarters happened to be in the same city where I had my surgery! I firmly believed I was now on the right path to a better future.

To get started, I realized I had to learn English—a daunting process. I remembered a conversation I had with a friend from high school, Carlos Tello, whose brothers had studied in the Soviet Union. Carlos told me that they'd learned Russian by studying and practicing every day. A year after their arrival, they successfully enrolled in college. If my friend's brothers could learn fluent Russian in a year, I should be able to do that with English. I would just have to work very hard.

I enrolled in English as a Second Language (ESL) courses at the Spanish Apostolate Center and dedicated myself to practicing English. A different volunteer helped during each two-hour shift. One of the volunteer tutors, a retired priest, had been the head of the English Department at Oxford University in England and, later, at Notre Dame College in Indiana. After tutoring me a few times, he told Sister Mary that he was impressed by my determination to learn English and volunteered to give me one-on-one ESL instruction. I had two-hour classes with him daily. To have a priest as a tutor seemed like yet another miracle, an assurance of God's presence.

I also studied with the assistance of volunteer readers and practiced speaking and reading English several hours a day. To familiarize myself with the sound of the language, I listened to the radio and television. The effort exhausted me and gave me frequent headaches.

Eileen called several times with updates about the possibility of training in the alternative skills of blindness, either at one of the NFB centers located in Louisiana, Colorado, and Minnesota, or at the state rehabilitation agency for the blind in New Mexico, where several staff members spoke Spanish. Eventually, we decided on New Mexico. The Executive Director there, Fred Schroeder, was from Peru, and he was more than happy to help me get training. My first reaction was that the name "Schroeder" did not sound Peruvian at all. It surprised me that someone from Peru just happened to be the director of the program that best suited my needs.

To show our appreciation for her help, Mama and I invited Eileen to dinner. Our cramped apartment had no living room or dining area, only a small round table in the kitchen. The night Eileen came over, the air was heavy with the savory aroma of spicy Peruvian food.

Eileen sniffed the air and took in the aroma as she came

into the apartment. "That smells wonderful! What are you cooking?"

"It's lomo saltado." Mama said with pride. Lomo saltado is my favorite meal—beef steak tips, tomatoes, and onions stir-fried in red wine vinegar and soy sauce, served with aji amarillo chili (a hot sauce), with rice and french fries.

Before dinner started, Eileen excused herself to wash her hands. Mama took the opportunity to tell me more about our guest. "Carlos, she looks so professional, very sharp and well-dressed."

I mentally adjusted my thoughts about the kind of work she did. Evidently, she did not work in a sheltered workshop. I would have to ask her more about that later.

Eileen came back to the dinner table, and we continued our conversation in Spanish. To Mama's great pleasure, Eileen lavishly praised her cooking. We relaxed and just enjoyed the conversation.

But, as the evening progressed, I wanted to know more. "What kind of job do you do?" I spoke hesitantly, not wanting to seem too intrusive.

Eileen said she worked as the administrative director of the Johns Hopkins Low Vision Research and Rehabilitation Center. I listened in shocked silence, my preconceptions shattering in my mind. She told me about her master's degree in business administration from the Wharton School of Business and her active involvement in the NFB. As she modestly described her accomplishments, I could hardly contain my great respect and wonder.

Then she turned the conversation back to me. As we all enjoyed a second helping of lomo saltado, she asked about my blindness and my goals. I told her about the detective academy, the struggles I had with the Ministry of Interior and police administration, my training at CERCIL. Because she seemed genuinely interested in my life and accomplishments,

I went on to share about my adventures selling products from Tacna, my acceptance to law school at San Martin University, how I met several blind people in Peru, and my hopes of eventually bringing Cati to America.

Eileen did not seem to think my goals were unrealistic at all. In fact, she encouraged me to learn English and to think about attending college in America with the goal of securing a good job. Her confidence in me, and in my abilities as a blind person, overwhelmed me a bit. Even as I voiced my dreams, I wavered in my belief in them. Eileen's support gratified me, but part of me still worried that I might fall short of my goals and wind up disappointing her and others. I was in a strange country with a different culture trying to learn a new language.

"Do you really think I could be as successful as you and others like you?" I asked, wanting to believe it could be true. Did I dare to dream like this? Her response reassured me—and inspired me as well.

"Don't worry, Carlos. One step at a time. First things first. Finish your training on blindness skills and concentrate on learning English. Do that, and you will be ready to consider what comes next. If that includes college and career, I don't see why not."

After Eileen left, I remained quiet, thinking about what just happened, and Mom thanked God for sending her to us. Her encouragement motivated me when I needed it most. It often seemed like I was struggling—both mentally and emotionally—all the time. Sometimes, I felt inadequate, like it was all too much for me. Was it really realistic for me to think I could learn English, attend college and then graduate school, and pursue a professional career as a blind person?

God's patience with me astounds me, looking back on it. He continued to bring people into my life to help me on my journey. He went before me, guiding me along—even though I didn't see it sometimes. I realized I just needed to trust Him. But occasionally I still felt downcast. I missed Cati and longed to have her with me. But I had much to accomplish before that could happen.

• Chapter Seventeen •

MIRACLES?

I made good progress in my ESL classes at the Spanish Apostolate. As we spent time together and got to know each other better, my tutor, the retired priest, became increasingly interested in my situation. When Sister Mary told me he wanted to know more about my training and ways to help me, I gave her Eileen's number. The priest spoke with Eileen and some of his friends to see what help might be available. Then Eileen called to tell me that the priest offered to sponsor me for my student visa to attend college. Sponsorship is critically important for people who wish to immigrate to the United States. Sponsors are financially responsible for the immigrant and must prove to the Immigration and Naturalization Service (now Citizenship and Immigration Services) that they are able to support the immigrant.

His generous offer seemed too good to be true. The

following afternoon, I asked Sister Mary to translate when the priest and I met for our session to make sure I'd understood everything correctly. The three of us sat at the table.

"Well, Carlos," Sister Mary said at the start of the meeting, "your tutor is very impressed with your determination and progress. He knows that Eileen is helping you arrange for training first in New Mexico."

Then Sister Mary began translating for the priest. Through her, he told me that he had spoken with officials at Notre Dame University and they had offered me a scholarship. I could start after I finished my training in the alternative skills of blindness in New Mexico.

I could hardly believe my incredibly good fortune. I had a sponsor and a scholarship to Notre Dame! The prospect thrilled me.

After the meeting. I wanted to express my gratitude more directly. "Thank you so much." I stuck out my left hand to shake his. The priest reached out to embrace me in a bear hug and patted my back. He was not a big man, maybe five-feet, three-inches tall, and thin. I returned his hug enthusiastically. Mama told me he had silver hair and blue eyes.

"You are an admirable young man. I just want to help if I can," the priest said. His unassuming, kind manner made him the sort of man who invited trust.

Was this a miracle? Mama certainly thought so when I told her about it later.

Eileen called to let me know that my training could start in a few weeks. Once in New Mexico, I could expect to become fully independent using the alternative skills of blindness. I would learn to read Braille, travel using a long white cane, and develop skills in the activities of daily living, computer operations, woodworking techniques, personal management, and advocacy skills.

I felt enormous gratitude for this totally unexpected

opportunity. I came to think of the priest as my personal benefactor, regarding him with special fondness, like an interested, if somewhat eager, family member. Surely God, who had promised to guide me, had sent this man to help.

The priest wanted to see for himself the training center in New Mexico, so he bought tickets for Mama and me to fly there with him. His generosity truly amazed me. Eileen gave me fifty dollars in donations from members of the Baltimore Chapter of the NFB. Sister Mary gave me one hundred dollars donated by one of the members of the church. Everything was coming together so well! It was like a dream! Maybe it really was a miracle after all.

We arrived in Albuquerque one sunny afternoon in early June. The dry air made the place feel noticeably different from Lima or Baltimore. Joe Cordova and Susan Benbow met us at the airport. Joe served as the deputy director of the New Mexico Commission for the Blind and was blind himself. Susan, an active member of the NFB of New Mexico, worked as a sighted special education teacher for blind children in the Albuquerque public schools. Both welcomed us warmly.

Joe spoke Spanish in an unfamiliar dialect. Some of the words he used reminded me of the old Spanish spoken by people in the Andes of Peru.

Mama described the sky as being more intensely blue and the sun brighter than in Baltimore or Lima. She described houses and buildings in the old adobe Spanish style. Instead of grassy lawns, gravel and rocks decorated most of the yards in front of the homes.

Joe lived in the southwest valley of Albuquerque. When we got to his house, his wife, Maria, welcomed us with enthusiasm, and they showed Mama her room. Then they took the priest and me to the room we would share. It had a couple of double beds. Joe wanted us to feel comfortable and told us to make ourselves at home and ask questions. He also expressed an interest in Peru.

Joe described rehabilitation training for the blind as a necessary prerequisite for excellence rather than mediocrity. In addition to being the Deputy Director of the New Mexico Commission for the Blind, he also served as the president of the NFB of New Mexico. He referred to the same articles by Dr. Jernigan that someone in Baltimore had given me. His passion about the many accomplishments of the NFB, especially in New Mexico, fired up my imagination.

The more I listened, the more I dreamed of being a part of the NFB, helping to open new opportunities for blind people everywhere.

That evening, Joe played his guitar and sang Spanish songs, such as "En El Rancho Grande," "De Colores," and so on. He served snacks and drinks. He and Maria were wonderful hosts and made us feel welcome. Joe's knowledge and wisdom about blindness and the NFB enthralled me. I wanted to be like him—content, in control of my life, independent, and productive.

The next morning, Joe, the priest, and I went to the New Mexico Commission for the Blind. The Commission had a workshop called New Mexico Industries for the Blind. Blind workers in the workshop used to be paid well below the minimum wage, received no benefits, and used obsolete equipment. In fact, in the past, they were not even called workers; they were called clients. Joe told me all of that changed when Fred Schroeder became the director of the New Mexico Commission for the Blind three years prior.

Under Fred's leadership, the workshop guaranteed blind workers at least the minimum wage and provided a full range of benefits, including vacation, retirement, and sick leave. The workshop replaced its obsolete equipment with modern, state-of-the-art machinery. Blind workers received training in the alternative skills of blindness and in the operation of the new, more efficient manufacturing equipment. They earned more money and had opportunities for advancement. Working conditions improved, and the workers were treated like other employees. The supervisors expected them to report to work on time, work hard, and stop using blindness as an excuse for idleness or poor work.

"Prevailing misconceptions about blindness are deeply rooted in societal attitudes," Joe said. "Most people have little or no experience with blind people, and what they think they know about us is based on gross misinformation. We are supposed to be sad, tragic figures, incapable of doing much for ourselves. Unfortunately, too many blind people accept these negative attitudes about blindness. We are part of society, after all, subject to societal conditioning like everyone else. If blind people, as a group, are expected to behave as if we were pitiful and helpless individuals, then many of us may behave in accordance with those expectations. We don't know enough to challenge our own misconceptions."

The next day at the commission building, Joe introduced me to Christine and Doug Boone, and my training on the alternative techniques of blindness began. Chris and I worked on reading and writing Braille; her husband, Doug, and I worked on travel using a long white cane. Though these were the same basic skills I learned at CERCIL, I quickly realized their approach to training differed radically.

It does not take long to learn the basic skills of blindness. They're pretty simple really. Within a few weeks, an individual can learn to write the Braille code and travel in familiar areas using a cane. However, instilling confidence in the application of those skills to participate fully in community life takes longer. Chris and Doug told me that if I faced a blindness-related problem, they expected me to not give up or look for help from others. I needed to figure out things on my own.

CERCIL used the "medical" or "traditional" model of

training, which focuses on the basic mechanical skills of blindness and little else. After two or three months at CERCIL, trainees often returned to sit at home as their skills slowly decayed through disuse because they lacked the confidence to engage in productive activity. They did not learn to believe in themselves as blind people.

In contrast, the Structured Discovery model approach employed in New Mexico involved the development of problem-solving skills and attitudinal adjustment promoting a more positive understanding of blindness and the potential of the blind. This model, a more philosophical, empowering approach than what I had known at CERCIL, went beyond the basic skills of blindness. My teachers expected me to develop independent action and problem solving.

At times, I felt overwhelmed absorbing all this new information, a new culture, and new people. I felt additional stress being away from my country and friends (especially Cati), learning the alternative techniques, and learning to understand and speak English in only one year to be accepted into college because of the medical visa expiration. Although I already had a scholarship offer and a sponsor, I still felt like I was running fast and could barely focus.

My English improved, but very slowly, it seemed. I struggled to understand what Chris and Doug tried to tell me. When all else failed, the priest would look up the correct references in his English-Spanish dictionary. Chris brought various objects to my attention, speaking the correct English word for each object presented. That helped me build my vocabulary and reinforced what I had already learned.

Doug told me that I should be able to carry a drink in my left hand while using my cane by holding it under my right arm. He expected me to figure it out on my own. With his encouragement, I found a technique that worked. This is just one example of the Structured Discovery method of blindness rehabilitation training in action.

I refused to let challenges related to my poor English or my one-handedness get in the way of my goal to live independently. Chris and Doug enjoyed helping me find alternative ways to function. Their professionalism and belief in blind people motivated me to work harder.

Unexpectedly, but happily, Mama met someone in Albuquerque and became engaged. Once she was satisfied that I was on track and making steady progress, she went back to Peru to retrieve the documents necessary to clear the way for her wedding.

Joe encouraged me to attend the NFB National Convention, to be held in Denver in July 1989. The New Mexico NFB affiliate would cover some of my expenses, and the priest volunteered to pay the rest. Joe also said the priest had confirmed my scholarship to Notre Dame and that he, the priest, would be my sponsor. I called my family in Peru and asked them to send my birth certificate and to have the required documentation translated and notarized. My dream of staying in America looked as though it might actually happen.

I would receive training at a well-respected rehabilitation center, my English improved each day, and I had a sponsor and a scholarship. Everything seemed to be going well—everything except for Cati. I had hoped she could come join me in America soon, but she had stopped communicating. I feared that our relationship might be over. The very idea filled me with dread.

One evening near the end of June, a week or so before the convention, the priest and I sat in our room, talking about how wonderful everyone had been—Fred Schroeder, Joe Cordova, Sister Mary, Eileen Rivera, and Chris and Doug Boone, especially. I expressed my sincere gratitude to the priest for his generous support. We talked about my plan to attend

Notre Dame for my undergraduate degree and the University of Oxford for my master's.

Then I started talking about Cati. At this point. the priest began acting strangely. He rose from his bed, where he had been reclining, and he stood at the foot of my bed while I sat with my back against the headboard. He told me of the powerful physical attraction he felt for me almost from the first time we met. Then he proposed that we have sex.

"What?" I exclaimed, feeling confused and alarmed.

He took out his dictionary and searched for the Spanish words to explain what he wanted. I hadn't misunderstood him.

I interrupted his search for words. "I am sorry, but I am not homosexual." The situation seemed totally bizarre.

"Then why do you hug me the way you do?" the priest persisted, pacing the floor, full of nervous energy.

"I am sorry you took my actions the wrong way," I said in halting English, trying to sound calmer than I felt. "In Peru, it's not unusual for men to hug each other as an expression of friendship. It does not mean we are homosexual. I think of you as the grandfather I never had."

"I am not a substitute!"

"And I am not homosexual," I said firmly.

The priest abruptly left the room at this point, leaving me stupefied. What had just happened here? With a sinking feeling in my gut, I struggled to make sense of it. This felt unreal, like a nightmare. The priest did not come back into the room until very late that night. Neither one of us said anything about what had happened.

The next day, the priest seemed awkward and unsure of himself. Maybe he feared I might expose his indiscretion to others. To reassure him, I told him that so long as we understood each other, we could still be friends. I would not say anything about it to anyone else. The priest seemed to relax, and we began talking to each other as if nothing had happened.

Once we got over that hurdle, however, I became curious. I asked him how he had managed to hide his sexuality from others, especially from those in the church. He admitted that it wasn't easy. Homosexuality was widely regarded as a personal failing. He had avoided detection so far, but it was a stressful way to live.

A few days later, the priest told Joe that something had come up and he needed to return to Baltimore. A couple of weeks after that, he changed his number and Joe could no longer reach him. I knew Joe felt confused, but I didn't tell him about what had transpired between the priest and me. Sadly, my dreams of Notre Dame and Oxford evaporated like a cloud, but I couldn't worry about it. I had other, more urgent things to think about.

In that strange season, I began to have a recurring dream, in which I ran down cold, dimly lit streets. After a few steps, my legs would feel heavy and, then, nearly impossible to move. A shadowy figure pursued me, and I felt as if I were trying to run through deep mud or quicksand. I'd awaken, gasping for air, my heart racing. Each time I had the dream, I wondered what, if anything, it meant or the relevance it had to my life.

My visa would expire in two months, and I needed to apply for an extension. What would I do after my training in New Mexico? I no longer had a sponsor, and I still didn't know if I had a relationship with Cati anymore.

Cati later revealed to me that she had stopped communicating with me because the priest advised her by letter to do so. He told her that she would help me more if she refrained from communications for a while so I could better concentrate on my training and learning English. Otherwise, my preoccupation interfered with my ability to focus. He actually told Cati to end our relationship, for my sake, if she cared anything for me at all.

This revelation greatly upset me. I told Cati how her lack of communication hurt and confused me. She did not distract me; instead, she filled me with strength and inspiration. It took a while, but eventually our relationship was restored. Despite the miles between us, our hearts connected more deeply than ever.

Soon, I attended the NFB National Convention in Denver— an amazing experience. More than 2,500 blind people from all over the world gathered for a full week to discuss every conceivable topic related to blindness. In the exhibit hall, vendors demonstrated cutting-edge technology and resources for blind consumers. The convention included seminars for blind students, blind teachers, blind lawyers, parents of blind children, and other special interest groups. I attended forums on national and international concerns and other presentations and workshops, soaking it all in.

The advanced access technology impressed me. I learned about computer screen readers (conversion of print displayed on the screen into audible speech), Braille embossers, different kinds of slates and styluses, a variety of white canes, Braille watches, and other specialized products. I learned about the Talking Book Program (a service of the National Library Service for the Blind and Print Disabled), and special four-track cassette recorders for the blind (capable of recording four times more information than could be recorded on standard cassette tapes).

Wherever I went, blind people of all ages and levels of independence, from every conceivable background and occupation, gathered like a large, close-knit family. I felt fortunate and happy to be part of such a positive, empowering gathering. During the convention, several deserving blind students received scholarships to help them achieve their professional goals. Anyone who could help did so. Everyone worked together with love, passion, and determination to achieve equality, opportunity, and security for blind people everywhere. I thrilled at the notion that dreams came true here.

At the opening session, the 2,500 federation members sat grouped by state. The atmosphere was charged with incredible energy! Attendees called out the names of their states to help people entering the ballroom find their delegations. I got goosebumps as I entered the ballroom and felt the rush of excitement, joy, and hope sweeping over me.

Because of my limited English, I didn't understand much of what went on. Joe Cordova translated as best he could. I appreciated his effort, but I knew his responsibilities as president of the New Mexico NFB affiliate kept him very busy and prevented him from giving me so much undivided attention and help. Despite the gaps in my understanding, I realized something of great significance was taking place. The history of the blind was being re-written, by blind people, for themselves.

Dr. Marc Maurer, president of the National Federation of the Blind, delivered two major addresses. On the opening day of the convention, he described the work of the federation over the past year. He confidently outlined how the NFB influenced and shaped national policy. Dr. Maurer gave his second major address at the closing banquet: a time of celebration and a time of reflection. I did not understand all of his words then, either, but what I did understand motivated me in a powerful way. Dr. Maurer called us to action. He gave us strength and hope. The destiny of the blind was up to us, he said. If we wanted freedom, we would have to take it; it would not be given to us. He repeatedly exhorted us to come together in a spirit of unity.

"We know who we are ... the future belongs to us ... let us act ... and we will make it all come true!" his voice thundered across the ballroom as people rose to give him a standing ovation that went on and on. It was thrilling. Intense emotions welled up inside me. I find it impossible to describe them adequately. More than ever, I knew that I wanted to be part of this fantastic organization where blind people took charge of their lives and their own destinies.

Back in New Mexico a couple of days later, I learned of an opening for me to begin my blindness skills training at the Orientation Center in Alamogordo, a small town one hour north of the Mexican border. Feeling energized and raring to go after the NFB National Convention, I prepared for the next chapter in my life.

• Chapter Eighteen •

THE TRAINING CENTER

Gladys Martinez, my vocational rehabilitation counselor, and I had visited the Orientation Center for the Blind in Alamogordo in June, a couple of weeks before the NFB national convention. Gladys, originally from Puerto Rico, spoke Spanish. Although I knew New Mexico was dry, Gladys helped me appreciate just how arid it really was through her descriptions of how vegetation, animal life, and even housing around us changed as it became drier the further south we drove. She also told me how the atomic bomb was tested in Alamogordo and about the reputed sighting of aliens at nearby Roswell. It surprised me that so far away from Peru, New Mexico had towns with Spanish names, such as Los Lunas, Ruidoso, Las Cruces, and so on.

This time, I traveled by myself. It took about four hours on the bus to get to Alamogordo, plenty of time to mull over my situation and wonder how things might turn out. Can I really learn enough English to be accepted as a foreign student? Will I find a sponsor? How will I support myself until I get a work permit and a job?

I knew if I buckled down and worked hard I could learn English well enough to be accepted to college. I was less certain about getting a student visa and work permit. For that, I needed a sponsor, and I had no idea where to find one. The more I thought about my situation, the less certain my future seemed.

I sat on the bus staring—without seeing—out the window. I thought about my life growing up in the San Juan neighborhood of Lima and how drastically things had changed after my accident. My mood was somber, but I was determined to move forward with my life.

I arrived in Alamogordo on a very hot and dry Sunday afternoon in July, filled with anticipation and self-doubt. My classes would start the next day. My English was still shaky. I feared I would not be able to meet the teachers' expectations.

The Orientation Center was divided into two parts, a classroom building and a dormitory. The administrator, secretary, gym, woodworking shop, and two field service counselors were located on the first floor of the classroom building. The personal management, home management, Braille, and communications (computers and access technology for the blind) rooms were on the second floor. The dormitory was located just east of the main classroom building—with men housed on the west end; a communal living room, kitchen, and dining room were situated in the middle. Women resided on the southeast end.

Richard Davis, the Orientation Center administrator, was professional, serious, and formal, but his patience and obvious care for center students inspired trust.

When we first met, Dick said, "Carlos, other than being a

detective, if you were not blind, what would you like to do?"

"I would like to be an attorney or an administrator." I had been asked the question many times before and no longer needed to think about my answer.

"Great! We will help you become a lawyer or administrator." He gently squeezed my upper arm near my shoulder.

I was stunned by his answer. Before meeting Eileen Rivera, Joe Cordova, and now Dick Davis, no other blindness professional had ever expressed so much confidence in me and in my abilities. I assumed he would be reserved and skeptical about my ability to achieve such ambitious goals. I needed to adjust my expectations about this place. Clearly, if I said I was going to do something, I'd better be prepared to back it up with action.

The familiar sound of a slate and stylus interrupted my thoughts. Dick was writing Braille with a slate and stylus. That was not unusual in and of itself—I was learning to do the same—but Dick was the only sighted person I had ever met who knew Braille. After a minute or so, Dick handed me my Braille schedule. I was surprised and impressed. I would not have expected a sighted person to be comfortable using a slate and stylus and acting as though it were entirely normal. My estimation of his leadership rose even higher. More surprises soon followed.

I learned that five of the eight instructors were blind. CERCIL had only one blind instructor—the Braille teacher.

At the time I began my training, the Orientation Center was nearing the end of its transition from a traditional medical model to the Structured Discovery model of blindness skills training. I found all but one of the instructors to be approachable and supportive and have positive attitudes about blindness and high expectations.

From the start, I knew I should spend a significant amount of time in the Orientation Center, but I worried the staff and students might not easily accept me because of my poor English. Fortunately, my fears were quickly dispelled. Everyone made me feel comfortable and welcome. Well, everyone except for Dan, the Braille instructor.

Dan, who'd worked at the center for a very long time, opposed—in a passive-aggressive manner—the change in teaching philosophy and the reforms Dick had put in place. Dan said he could not teach me Braille because he was a Braille instructor, not an ESL teacher. I already knew the Braille alphabet and most of the contractions from my training at CERCIL and from Chris Boone. Even so, on my first day in his class, Dan gave me only four letters in Braille to read: A, B, C, and D. I tried to explain that I already knew the Braille alphabet and many contractions, but he pretended not to understand. Then he insisted that he had his own method of teaching Braille, and that was what he would use. For the entire week, Dan refused to give me more than the first four letters of the alphabet.

A couple of weeks later, Dan learned that I was practicing Braille in my room, using a Braille book, Braille paper, a slate and stylus, and a Perkins Brailler (also called a Braillewriter, a manual device for typing Braille). Thinking that someone was teaching me Braille on the sly, he angrily protested that he was the only one with the necessary credentials to teach Braille. But no one was teaching me Braille. A teacher had helped me get what I needed to practice on my own, that was all. Later, I learned Dick Davis knew of my self-study and supported it. As far as I was concerned, Dan could rant and rave all he wanted. I just ignored him.

The pressure to learn English was intense. A student visa was the only way I could stay in America. That meant I needed to know enough of the language to be accepted into a university. In the meantime, I also needed to learn more of it to fully benefit from my training.

I always did something to improve my English. I took notes with a slate and stylus or tape recorder. I practiced handwriting with a pen attached to my prosthetic right hand. I developed one-handed keyboarding methods for the type-writer, computer keyboard, and Braillewriter. To build my vocabulary, I learned ten to twenty new words every day. In each of my classes, I asked the teacher the meaning and spelling of the words I heard most often.

I touched different objects, asked what they were and how they were spelled, wrote the words in Braille with my slate and stylus, and repeated them several times to commit them to memory. Then I used the Braillewriter to write sentences using those words. To practice handwriting, I used paper with raised lines and a pen held in the hook on my right hand. Then, as the communications teacher corrected my spelling and grammar, I would rewrite them correctly in Braille. After that, I would record myself reading the corrected sentences out loud. Finally, I would listen to the recording while following along in Braille. That allowed me to practice my pronuncia-tion, spelling, and Braille all at the same time.

At CERCIL, I was told a Braillewriter required two hands to operate. I assumed the CERCIL instructor knew what could and could not be done. I never considered the possibility that he might be wrong. Things were entirely different in New Mexico. The Orientation Center instructors assumed just about every problem had a solution and encouraged imagi-nation and experimentation.

Braillewriters have six keys corresponding to the six dots that make up the Braille cell. A single dot in the upper left corner of the cell (dot one) represents the letter a. A single dot in the lower right corner of the cell (dot six) means the following letter is capitalized. The three keys to the left of the spacebar activate dots one, two, and three, which together constitute the left side of the cell. The three keys to the right of the spacebar activate dots four, five and six—the right side of the cell. There is also a key to the left of dot three to advance to the next line and a Backspace key to the right of dot six.

My communications teacher, Arlene Carr, encouraged me to try out different ways of using the Braillewriter keyboard with one hand. To get me started, she suggested methods she thought might work. From there, I began experimenting. It took a couple of days, and a bit of trial and error, to work it out. I ended up using the little, ring, and middle fingers of my left hand for the three keys to the left of the spacebar (dots three, two, and one, respectively). For the three keys to the right of it, I used the index finger of my left hand for the first key (dot four), the end of my right arm for the other two keys (dots five and six), and the thumb of my left hand for the spacebar itself. Just like Chris and Doug Boone, the communications instructor celebrated with me and encouraged me every time I found a solution to a problem. That motivated me to keep going whenever blindness or one-handedness presented a challenge.

Actually, using the Braillewriter was not nearly as difficult as using a typewriter or computer keyboard. As I mentioned, the Braillewriter has a key for each dot in the six-dot Braille cell, plus the spacebar, Line Advance key, and Backspace key—that's it. Learning to operate a typewriter or computer keyboard, with their multitude of keys, using only one hand proved much harder. In fact, I found it nearly as difficult as learning English.

Learning to use a typewriter or computer keyboard seemed impossible. But the communications instructor insisted it was no big deal; we just needed to find a system that worked efficiently. We tried many approaches, some mine and some hers, but nothing seemed to work. She refused to give up. As soon as it was clear a particular approach wasn't working, she smiled and cheerfully moved on, confident we would find a solution. Her determination and confidence kept me going.

I started with the traditional hand position: my little finger on the letter A, my ring finger on the letter S, and so on. Then, I would move my hand to the right side of the keyboard, place my index finger on the Semicolon key, my middle finger on the letter L and, so on. Moving my hand back and forth, looking for letters, numbers, and punctuation marks caused me to lose my place. No matter how hard I tried, I did not improve.

Still, the communications instructor would not let me give up. She loaned me a typewriter and told me to practice typing in my free time. For several evenings, I did so, but the problem persisted. When I got frustrated, I took a deep breath and vowed to keep trying. I understood the importance of this training, and I needed to make the most of the opportunity. Everyone at the New Mexico Commission for the Blind, especially the Orientation Center staff, cared about and believed in me. Their faith in me helped keep me focused. I was disheartened but determined. Given the increasing importance of computers in higher education and the labor market, I knew that my opportunities in America depended on good keyboarding skills. I had no choice but to keep at it.

After days of fruitless effort and frustration, something clicked. I put my hand on the middle of the keyboard with my little finger on the letter D and my index finger on the letter I. That allowed me to extend my little finger to the left, to the letters S and A and my index finger to the letters J, K, and L and the Semicolon. I could move up and down without losing my place. I was extremely pleased with myself for coming up with this innovation. Soon after my breakthrough, I was able to use the typewriter to practice spelling English words.

As I became more comfortable using the typewriter, I marked some of the keys with Braille dots to facilitate navigation to the left, right, up, and down, including numbers. The method transferred easily to the computer keyboard, with additional Braille dots to mark the Tab, Enter, and Control keys.

Computers made me especially nervous. Because I had never used a computer, I had an irrational fear I would do something wrong and cause irreparable damage. One day, the computer screen reader declared, "You have performed an illegal operation." That error message alarmed me! For days, I avoided that computer, afraid that the Immigration Service had been notified of my illegal activity and I would be deported to Peru. I had close calls in other classes, but nothing as distressing as that.

One day, I was about to put a tray of cookies in the oven, when the home management instructor stopped me. She reminded me of the steps I needed to follow to keep from burning myself. She was also blind. I admired her ability to function in the kitchen and monitor what I was doing at the same time. As a blind instructor, she was a powerful role model, demonstrating what blind people can do using safe and effective nonvisual methods. She helped me understand that nonvisual skills worked just as well as sight—sometimes better. When blind people cannot do something, it is easy to blame blindness, but such an attitude perpetuates dependency. The home management instructor taught me to cook. Equally important, she taught me to take responsibility for myself and my own safety.

Two years of traveling as a blind person on the tough streets of Lima made me one of the best cane travelers in my orientation and mobility class. With the long white cane the NFB had given me in Baltimore, I was able to walk quickly and with confidence, just like I did before I became blind. The cane reached my chin and was far superior to the shorter, chest-high cane I used in Peru. The longer cane allowed me to detect objects at greater distances, which gave me more time to react. If I had had a long cane in Peru, I would not have fallen into the sewer line in my neighborhood.

Getting around in Peru was treacherous. In Lima, blind people had to contend with broken, uneven sidewalks with holes everywhere, garbage strewn about in some neighborhoods, and merchandise hanging from kiosks. Blind people also had to worry about crime in some parts of the city.

Alamogordo was much easier. The sidewalks were clean, wide, and even; the traffic was light, and drivers obeyed the traffic signals; people didn't jostle each other on the streets; and, to my relief, the crime rate was very low.

I did so well in orientation and mobility that I finished the class early, and my instructor asked me to help teach other students. Finishing cane travel also allowed me to spend more time in the computer class.

The Orientation Center program included a woodworking or industrial arts class along with all other classes. At first, it seemed odd that I should have to learn woodworking. Other more practical skills like cooking and Braille seemed more important. But I soon found that wood shop was about far more than teaching woodworking. It was about building self-confidence and the belief that blind people can learn new things. When blind people learn to use power tools safely, it gives them the confidence to face other challenges in life. At first, I doubted I could operate power tools safely and independently, but I was quickly converted. In almost no time, I believed I could do anything I needed to do to take care of ordinary home repairs using manual and power tools.

Occasionally, a student would make fun of my accent or poor English, but not often. For the most part, the students were open and friendly, the classes were fun and engaging, and the instructors were supportive and caring.

I spent my evenings and weekends practicing English and

Braille, but I progressed slowly. I struggled with simple conversations in English or reading stories in Braille. I felt intense pressure because I could feel time literally slipping away from me. In less than ten months, I had to be ready to take the foreign student English examination. In addition, my visa would expire in a month, and I had good reason to worry about what the immigration service might do. Except for meals, I spent very little time with the other students.

Around 7:00 p.m. one evening, I was in my room studying when someone knocked on my door. I was surprised because I didn't encourage people just to drop by and socialize. Curious, I opened the door and heard footsteps running away. I thought one of the students who liked to make fun of my accent was playing a prank, but I heard women's voices coming from down the hall.

I stepped into the hall where I heard a woman say, "Carlos, come talk to us."

"I am sorry, but I am studying English," I replied apologetically, walking up to them, not wanting them to think I didn't care for their company. "I don't have much time to get ready for the English exam," I added.

"If you don't practice your English talking to us, how in the world do you think you will ever get any good at it? Come to the student lounge so you can hear us talking and you can work on your pronunciation—because you need practice!" She sounded as if she were chastising a little brother.

The woman, Veronica Smith, was right. She made me realize that my self-imposed isolation made it harder to develop conversational English. I needed to be with people, make mistakes, and hear how others spoke in a variety of social situations. I began spending more time making friends and, not surprisingly, my English improved considerably.

But we used our social time for more than conversation. We used the time to practice and reinforce our nonvisual skills. When I discovered I was particularly good at teaching Braille and cane travel, I considered becoming a blindness skills instructor. I enjoyed helping others and thought that perhaps I could support myself and pay for college by teaching.

As people spoke, I still mentally translated the English to Spanish. That made it difficult to follow conversations. I needed to get over that hurdle. I made a conscious effort to stop translating in my mind, but it was easier said than done.

I found numbers and simple math especially difficult in English. I decided to count only in English until it was natural. When the orientation and mobility instructor gave me a travel assignment, I counted my footsteps until I reached one thousand. Before long, I could count in English with relative ease.

By the way, many people believe that blind people memorize the number of steps from one place to another. I suppose it is possible that some blind people count steps, but it would be unreliable and impractical. What would happen if the blind person needed to make a detour or lost count? It is far better to be aware of where you are in relation to your surroundings.

Once I was comfortable counting in English, I decided to use the same method to build my vocabulary. I repeated English words to myself over and over and spent more time listening to the news. Slowly, I was able to follow a conversation in English without mentally translating it. Then I had a dream in English. Upon waking, it was a little disturbing, but then I realized that meant learning and using English was finally coming more naturally.

One Saturday morning in September, Mr. Davis came to my room to inform me that there was a letter for me from the Immigration and Naturalization Service. The day I had been dreading had arrived. I took the envelope with trepidation and noticed it hadn't been opened. I asked Mr. Davis to open the envelope, and, if he would be so kind, to read the letter to me. The first few paragraphs consisted of general information, increasing my alarm. I thought bad news was sure to follow, but, to my immense relief, I was wrong. My visa had been extended for another year.

Later, when I informed Mr. Cordova that my visa had been extended, we agreed that this gave me more time to finish my training and improve my English in preparation for the college entrance examination. Mr. Davis supported the plan. He asked me if things were turning out the way I had hoped.

"Yes, Mr. Davis, it is very good news." I gave him a big smile. My English wasn't good enough to fully express my happiness, so that was all I could say.

The extension of my visa renewed my motivation and spirit. Dick, the students, and the instructors all noticed my positive attitude and confidence. That big stressor removed, I was happy and often joking around, even as I continued to work hard on my English and blindness skills.

One day, my cane travel instructor noticed I was tapping my cane tip too hard. In Peru, we do not have a cane tip factory, so we use heavy iron tips, which take a little more muscle. In the US, the cane tips are rubber. Only the end is metal. The US cane tips allow the entire cane to be lighter. In addition, they make a crisp tapping sound that enables the blind person to identify different surfaces and to hear how large a room is. The instructor showed me how to tap the cane tip lightly on the floor. She said, "See, it is like a kiss."

Smiling, I said, "The problem is, I am very passionate." Several of the students and teachers laughed. I suddenly realized I had not translated in my mind before answering. English was feeling more and more natural. However, reading books reminded me that I had a long way to go. I still did not know many words.

One afternoon, during home management class, my teacher said she would like to teach me some improper English words and expressions. I told her that I was not interested and had no time for that. "Well," she said, "if someone says, 'You son of a bitch,' don't say, 'Thank you,' or 'You are welcome.'" That got my attention!

At the end of September, Mr. Davis drove us to the National Federation of the Blind of Arizona state convention in Tucson. On the way, we stopped for a stretch break and took some pictures next to huge cactuses and marveled at how tall they were by touching them and asking Mr. Davis about them. When we got to Tucson, we went first to the home of a longtime leader of the NFB, James Omvig. Mr. Omvig and his wife lived in a beautiful house with a patio and swimming pool in the backyard. Before dinner, our host invited us for a swim in the pool. After a while, we relaxed with drinks on the patio. They served us cooked meats, vegetables, legumes, breads, and various sauces. We thoroughly enjoyed the warm, dry evening. The luxuriousness and spaciousness of this elegant home impressed me greatly. During dinner, Mr. Omvig was welcoming and gracious. I did not know how to start a conversation with such a well-educated man. As it turned out, I didn't have to.

He took the time to speak to each of us individually. Turning to me, he asked my name, where I was from, how long I had been in the United States, and so on. I replied simply and without elaboration. Intimidated by this impressive man, I wanted him to think well of me, and I feared my limited English would make a poor impression.

Then Mr. Omvig asked, "What would you like to do after you finish your training?" He spoke with the same warm, encouraging voice he used with the other students.

I gave him the same answer I had been giving people who asked this question for some time. "I want to go to law school to become a lawyer or administrator."

Interested, Mr. Omvig leaned closer and told me that he

was a lawyer himself and had been a lawyer for the Social Security Administration, had worked as the deputy director of the Iowa Commission for the Blind, and had directed the Alaska Center for Blind Adults, a private agency in Anchorage. I was thrilled to meet a blind person who had been a successful lawyer in the US. Then he asked me how I became blind, what I had done before coming to America, and how I wound up in Alamogordo.

"Your English is very good for someone who has been in this country for only a few months." He exuded warmth and sincerity.

"I am not sure how I will do in college and law school, since English is not my first language. I still have a long way to go, and I'm sure the level of English expected of me will be higher and harder." I hoped he wouldn't laugh.

I was surprised when he put his right hand on my left shoulder and said encouragingly, "Carlos, I've been around a good deal, and I know a lot of blind people, and I am confident you can accomplish anything you put your mind to. Just continue being as determined as you have been and finish your training."

I assured him I would, thanked him, and, feeling more at ease, asked him about his professional life. "When you were young, did you have doubts about achieving your goals?" I asked.

"Carlos, we all have doubts when we are young, and especially when we are blind. The key is good training in blindness skills, and you are in a very good training center. Don't lose sight of your goals. Surround yourself with positive people and good blind role models," he replied, emphasizing each word, making sure I would remember his words for the rest of my life.

I asked him which university he attended, how he took notes, and how he operated in a courtroom. After answering my questions, he talked about the work he did for the Social Security Administration, the Iowa Commission for the Blind, and the Alaska Center for Blind Adults. I was impressed by his remarkable career and eloquence and moved by his personal interest in me. He had just met me, but he demonstrated absolute faith in my ability to succeed.

As winter approached, the weather turned cold. One day, the temperature dropped to 32°F, much colder than Lima, but I had other things on my mind. I was worried about my lack of finances, when one of my instructors asked if I would be interested in cleaning the courthouse. Actually, I thought she said, "horse house." I pictured myself cleaning out a stable. But it didn't matter. I was desperate for money and immediately said, "Yes." As she told me more about the work, I realized she was talking about an office building, not a stable. At home, I cleaned my room, washed windows, cleaned the bathroom, and dusted furniture. But I had never cleaned an entire building. I was apprehensive but grateful for the opportunity to make some money. It occurred to me that, if my instructor believed in me, I could believe in myself. It gave me confidence. As it turned out, cleaning the courthouse was not as difficult as I had feared.

Plastic bags lined the wastebaskets. All I had to do was change out the bags and carry the trash to the dumpster in the alley. Most of the building was carpeted, so I only needed to vacuum the floors. I used a chemical spray and paper towels to polish the furniture. The restrooms were cleaned the same way, except I used a disinfectant spray. I did all this wearing rubber gloves and a mask. I cleaned the building twice a week, two hours each time. I made six dollars an hour, one dollar and seventy-five cents above minimum wage. It was great! I made a little money while going through training. I also enrolled in ESL classes that met two evenings a week. My self-esteem grew, and my future looked more and more promising.

Life was going well. My English was improving. I had friends, and people treated me well. And I was busy. I had every reason to be optimistic, but I was homesick. I missed the culture, the food, the traditions, the language, my family, my friends, and especially Cati.

I could do little to relieve my homesickness. Although I missed her and wanted to talk to her, Cati's father had ordered her to break off the relationship and would not allow her to call me. Back then, international calls were very expensive, so I only called once a month. I asked Mr. Davis if I could use the Orientation Center phone. He checked with the state office in Santa Fe and received permission. I could use his office phone as long as I paid for the calls. After each one, an operator would call back and tell me the cost.

When I placed my first call to Cati, I was excited, but, to my great disappointment, someone else answered the phone. Cati was not there. To add insult to injury, the operator told me that the international connection cost five dollars and the one-minute call was an additional three dollars. I tried calling Cati again over the next few days. On the third attempt, I finally reached her. I could tell she couldn't speak freely and was pretending she was talking to someone else. I didn't care. I was happy to listen to her voice and to hear her say, "Me, too," when I said I loved and missed her. The call was worth it, even though it cost around thirty-five dollars for a ten-minute call that went way too fast.

Separation from Cati was brutal. Our calls were not frequent or long enough, and they took most of my money. I missed her more after every call. I would tell her the date and time of my next call, so she could be ready to answer the phone, but that didn't always work. It was expensive and frustrating.

One day, as I failed to reach Cati yet again, an instructor saw what I was going through. She said maybe I would have better luck if I called in the evening. But I couldn't use any of the agency's phones after 5:00 p.m. The instructor offered to let me use her credit card, so I could call from a pay phone.

I gratefully accepted. I called Cati's aunt's house. Her aunt lived next door, and I thought it might be easier to reach Cati if I called there. But that was not to be. Her aunt answered the phone, and, when she realized I was trying to reach Cati, she made it clear in a cordial but firm tone that I was not to call again.

"All you are doing is getting her in trouble with her father. You know he is opposed to the relationship. Please leave her alone and stop calling." Then she hung up.

The instructor was standing nearby. "What happened? Why did you hang up?" she asked.

Dejected and struggling to control my emotions, I told her about the call. She listened sympathetically. She was easy to talk to. Perhaps it was because she had children of her own who were in college and close to my age. She said she was sure I would find a way to reach Cati. It was hard, but it would have been much harder if she hadn't been there to support me.

As I thought about the immigration process and my need for a sponsor, my brain worked overtime. And those were not my only worries. When my training ended, I would have nowhere to live, and I'd be unemployed. Add to that my inadequate language skills and my aching homesickness. Still, I didn't complain. I had not come to the United States assuming that everything would just fall into place. I knew it would be tough going. I thought to myself, Well, here I am. And, sure enough, it is just as tough as I imagined it would be.

I was set to graduate in a few weeks and needed to find somewhere to live. With Joe Cordova's help, I enrolled at the Technical Vocational Institute (TVI) in Albuquerque (now Central New Mexico Community College). ESL classes were free. All I had to worry about was work, rent, food, and a sponsor for college—no sweat. Yeah, right.

I wanted to help my blind friends in Peru, so I organized a raffle. Many of the instructors and students bought tickets and also helped sell them. On several cold Sunday mornings, I stood by the entrance to the Catholic Church to sell tickets. Altogether, we raised $500. I used the money to buy reams of Braille paper and dozens of slates and styluses. The problem was how to send all this to Peru without paying for shipping. The solution would come later.

I graduated from the Orientation Center in early January 1990. I wrapped up my training ahead of schedule, so I could start ESL classes in Albuquerque the following week. Once again, I could not help but compare the training at CERCIL with the Orientation Center. The Orientation Center staff believed in blind people and demonstrated it in their every action. CERCIL instructors were condescending and offered little hope for a productive future.

The day before I left for Albuquerque, the Orientation Center students presented me with a gift. They had taken up a collection and bought a backpack for me to use in college. I was profoundly moved. Graduating students, myself included, faced an uncertain future. But with the skills and confidence we gained and the friendships we made, we faced that future with optimism. I would miss their daily kindness and encouragement, but the ties we had formed were strong. To this day—thirty-two years later —a number of them remain good friends.

I reflected back over the months since I had arrived in the United States. I thought about the many struggles and obstacles I had experienced and knew I should be grateful and happy things were working out so well. After all, I was in America and well on my way to a new life. But I still had doubts. I had worked hard and would keep working hard, but at times my future seemed as stark and uninviting as the landscape of the moon, or New Mexico, if you prefer. It made me feel dispirited and a bit sorry for myself, but I could not indulge my doubts for long. I could not afford to waste time dwelling on what might have been. I needed to face the next chapter in my life—with hope, determination, and confidence.

• Chapter Nineteen •

THE STRANGER IN THE HALLWAY

The Orientation Center held a special dinner for the graduating students on the last Friday of training in Alamogordo. That afternoon, I said my goodbyes to my friends and teachers. The next day, Dick Davis invited the students and staff to his home for lunch. The fact that the Orientation Center Director would open his home to us made a lasting impression. Other things he did, like hiring center students to occasionally babysit his three young children, showed how much he trusted us. His belief in blind people elevated our self-esteem and belief in ourselves. That day, he told me that if I needed a letter of recommendation, he would be more than glad to write one.

My most immediate concern was finding a way to support myself. Under immigration law, people who come to the United States for medical reasons like I did must obtain a time-limited B-2 Medical Visitor Visa. These visas do not allow foreign nationals to work. The janitorial work I did during my Orientation Center training was arranged as part of my rehabilitation program. The work experience was very short term and was meant to promote self-confidence. The immigration office would not have approved it otherwise.

My ESL classes started the second week of January, right after I returned to Albuquerque from Alamogordo. Joe Cordova told me his cousin Philip was willing to share his apartment with me. Philip was also blind and worked for Industries for the Blind in Albuquerque. He lived with his niece and her baby in a low-income apartment with one bedroom, a small living room, and a kitchen. We agreed that my stay would be temporary—only until I could find a place of my own. Philip's niece and her baby slept in the bedroom, Philip slept on a foam mattress on the floor, and I slept on the sofa. In the mornings, we stored the foam mattress in a closet to make more space in the living room. Now, I just had to worry about food.

Of course, Philip and his niece could not provide me with three meals a day, like I had at home, the detective academy, or the Orientation Center. Philip was kind enough to share his breakfast and dinner with me, for which I was very grateful. During the day, Philip was away at work, so I was on my own for lunch. I only had one hundred dollars, money I needed for a deposit on an apartment, so I skipped lunch and concentrated on studying English.

Three weeks later, a studio apartment opened for occupancy in the same large complex where Philip and his family lived. The complex was located in southeast Albuquerque, between Kathryn and Cesar Chavez avenues, a block east of Yale Boulevard. It had several buildings and a common laundry facility.

I felt fortunate that a small, inexpensive studio apartment had become available. The deposit was fifty dollars and my rent was eighty dollars a month, including utilities. That was more money than I had just then, but the commission had agreed to help with living expenses for a few months until I could manage it. I had a bathroom, kitchen, and a combination dining room, living room, and bedroom. By American standards, it was small, but it was the largest space I had ever had for myself. To my surprise, the kitchen came complete with cabinets, a refrigerator, a stove with gas already connected, and a garbage disposal. It was a low-income apartment in America. In Peru, it would have been a studio apartment for an upper-middle-class person.

I now had a place to live, but I still needed groceries. Gladys Martinez, my rehabilitation counselor, helped me complete the application for assistance from Catholic Social Services. On the form, I indicated the nature and extent of my need for assistance as including, in addition to groceries, a cooking pot, a fork, a spoon, a knife, a bowl, a plate, and a coffee cup. Gladys faxed the completed application form to Catholic Social Services. Then she called to confirm that the form had been received and to find out what would happen next. They told her that my case would be evaluated for the next couple of days. She was told that someone would be coming around soon to visit me in my apartment to verify my needs. That done, I moved into my new place with a cardboard box containing everything I owned: a couple of pairs of pants, a few pairs of underwear, a couple of shirts, my combination radio/tape recorder, and materials for writing Braille.

That evening, I was sitting alone in my apartment when the doorbell rang, surprising me. I was not expecting anyone.

"Who is it?" I asked, opening the door.

"My name is Tony," he said politely. "I'm with Catholic Social Services. I am here to confirm your need for groceries."

I invited him into my empty apartment, suddenly embarrassed about my lack of furniture and meager accommodations but happy about the rapid response. Tony switched to Spanish when he heard my heavily accented English.

He went right to work. Going first for the kitchen, I could tell by the noise he made that he was looking inside the refrigerator and rummaging through the cabinets to see what I had on hand.

"It looks like you need a few things," he said.

Then he went to the closet where I kept the cardboard box with my belongings and looked inside. "Hmm. You also need some winter clothes."

Standing in the middle of the room and looking around, Tony asked, "Where do you sleep?"

"Well, on the floor. I use my pants as a pillow."

He walked around the studio one more time, checking to make sure he hadn't missed anything. "I'll be back with a few things," he said abruptly and left the apartment, leaving me standing there stunned.

I had no idea what to think, what to expect, or what to do. When would he come back? I had no one to talk to about what just happened. I didn't have a phone. I felt lonely and unsure about my current situation, not to mention my future.

Tony came back a couple of hours later with another gentleman. Not wasting any time, they quickly carried in a sofa. They went about their business as if they were thoroughly enjoying themselves. They also brought in a couple of chairs, a couple of bowls, a couple of plates, utensils, and enough groceries for the next two weeks. They brought in cooking pots, a frying pan, a coffee maker, and a ladle. They gave me a warm jacket, shirts, warm pants, and a pillow. Everything had been used, but it was all in excellent condition.

Tony and his partner were incredible. From what they said, I figured that they were probably around sixty years old. Apparently, they did this sort of thing for Catholic Social Services quite a bit.

"How can I thank you guys?" I tried to tell them in Spanish. "I can hardly believe it."

Ten minutes earlier, I had nothing. Now I had everything I needed. It was as if God sent these men in my time of need.

"No problem, Carlos, this is what we do," Tony said modestly as they got ready to leave. "We will be back after we find a bed and a mattress."

To my surprise, Philip stopped by later that evening. He said that he had been in his hometown north of Santa Fe over the weekend and only found out about my move after he got back and his niece told him. Philip asked me if he could move in if he paid one hundred dollars a month for rent, the same amount he had been paying his niece. I was glad to have him for a roommate, but I told him that he would have to pay only forty dollars a month, half of my eighty dollars for rent.

Philip was a great roommate. Not only did I save on rent, but we split the cost of groceries and cleaned the apartment together. We became good friends.

Actually, we didn't really do that much together. I spent most of my time studying and getting ready for college. Phillip knew that I believed that a college education and hard work would prepare me for a career and a productive life. This motivated him to attend college too, but he needed alternative skills training first. Philip had been blind from birth and already possessed many of the fundamental skills of blindness, but he didn't have the opportunity to develop problem-solving skills or build self-confidence in himself as a blind person— skills he could get at a training center. In April, he left to attend the Orientation Center in Alamogordo.

Meanwhile, I headed off in a different direction for school. People from all around the world took ESL classes at the Albuquerque Technical Vocational Institute (TVI). I had no idea America was so diverse and was amazed to meet people from so many different countries.

My classes began at 8:00 in the morning and finished at 7:30 at night. Each was two hours long, and I had a break from 3:30 p.m. to 5:30 p.m. TVI provided readers to help me study during the break. The ESL program was organized into three parts—beginning, intermediate, and advanced. Each part was divided into three levels. I registered for the first level of intermediate ESL. If everything went as planned, I would move to level two by February and level three by March. My goal was to complete the third level of advanced ESL by June and be ready to take the examination for foreign students in early July. Since the fall semester started in mid-August, I would have to study hard to be ready. I continued listening to the news on the radio to get used to the sound of English. I practiced spelling by Brailling all my ESL lessons. It seemed like all I did was study, but I was determined to succeed.

I still needed a sponsor. Joe Cordova told me about Luis Santa Maria. Luis, who was from Peru, worked for a Spanish radio station and had a weekend television show on the Spanish channel. Joe thought that perhaps he might sponsor me. On my next visit to Joe's office, we called Luis. He was very friendly, but honest. He told me that he could not sponsor me and did not know anyone who could. However, he said he would come to Joe's office the following week to talk more.

When the three of us got together, Joe explained my situation. I was living and going to school in the US legally, and the Commission for the Blind was ready to support me in college and cover the cost of my tuition and books, but I needed a sponsor to get a student visa.

I told Luis that my mother had just married an American citizen. She had already applied to become a permanent resident and had listed me as a family member whom she hoped to have join her in the US. The problem was time. It would take several years before my mother's residency could be established and she could bring other family members to America.

Luis, who headed up a salsa band, was moving to Miami where they had a better chance of becoming internationally known. He said he would try to do what he could for me, but he might not have enough time to talk to his contacts before leaving.

Luis was about to make a trip back to Peru where he would be featured on several television programs promoting his band. I immediately thought of my blind friends in Lima and the materials I had collected for them—Dick Davis had brought them to Albuquerque a few weeks earlier. I asked Luis if he would be willing to take Braille paper, slates and styluses, and cassette tapes with articles in Spanish to Peru with him. I knew I was asking a lot, but I also knew my blind friends needed those things. When Luis hesitated, I was afraid he might not help. I told him that if he took the materials to Peru, he could say, during his television appearances, that he had brought materials from the United States to help the blind community in Peru. It would be sure to get the attention of the public and create a positive impression. He liked the idea. Laughing good-naturedly, he agreed to do as I asked. A few weeks later, I found out that everything got to where it was supposed to go. This made me feel good, knowing that I helped initiate something on behalf of the blind in Peru.

April came, and I still didn't have a sponsor. I urgently needed to find one, but how? The stress started getting to me. I had been having nightmares, and they were becoming more frequent. One recurring dream was particularly disturbing. A shadowy figure would open the door, silently come and stand over me in bed, wrap his iron fingers around my throat, and squeeze. I would wake up gasping for air, my heart thumping. I was only getting four to five hours of sleep a night.

Weeks passed with no sponsor and no hope of finding one. Without a sponsor, I was not eligible for a student visa. A couple of my female friends offered to marry me. Not only would that have been illegal, but also it would have made it impossible to reunite with Cati. I felt defeated. I was tired of trying and getting nowhere.

There are two kinds of student visas: F-1 and J-1. The F-1 student visa allows foreign students to attend US colleges and universities. F-1 student visa applicants must show that they have enough money to live on while they are studying in the United States, because the F-1 visa does not allow foreign students to work.

The J-1 student visa also allows foreign nationals to come to the United States to study. Generally, J-1 visa applicants are sponsored by a government agency. Students are required to maintain at least a B-plus average. The advantage of the J-1 visa is that students are allowed to work twenty hours a week during the semester and full-time during breaks.

I had all the paperwork, but it was worthless without a sponsor. Unless things changed and changed quickly, I would have to return to Lima.

Although I could feel my hopes for staying in the United States slipping away, I continued studying English. I thought that if I didn't get a student visa, I might still be able to teach English back in Peru. I found it ironic that I had never liked studying English, but now I was considering becoming an English teacher.

The end of May arrived, and I finished the intermediate level of ESL and the first two levels of advanced ESL. I still planned to complete advanced ESL in June so I could start the university's six-week English review class in July. People encouraged me to go ahead and take the English test for foreign students, but I was afraid I wasn't ready. Then I realized that if I went ahead and took the test, I would find out where I needed to improve. I could always retake the test.

The examination had four parts—a multiple-choice section, English conversation, finishing incomplete sentences, and writing a two-page essay. A professor from the university administered and read the two-hour test. Since I just wanted to learn my English proficiency level, I was not nervous and answered without hesitation. When the examination was finished, the professor congratulated me, told me I had passed, and said I was ready to start college. Both surprised and skeptical, I asked for my grade. The professor said that he had been scoring my performance as I finished each section and that my average was an A—a score of 98. I thanked him and left his office.

As I walked home that hot May afternoon, I had mixed feelings—I was pleased to have passed the test, but I also felt apprehensive. Classes would start in the middle of August, and I wasn't that confident in my English yet. Thankfully, I still had a couple of months to go before then to work on it. I had time to continue my ESL classes and practice.

Passing the foreign English examination removed a big obstacle, but the main one, the biggest one, the most difficult one remained—I still needed a sponsor to get a student visa.

After racking my brain for months, I had run out of ideas. The situation seemed hopeless. I couldn't see any kind of solution. I felt desperate. In spite of my determination, I had finally run up against a wall that I couldn't get past. There didn't seem to be anything more I could do.

One evening during a break in my ESL class at TVI, someone ran up to me in the hallway on my way back to class. "Hi. My name is Jim," he said. "I always see you taking classes and wanted to meet you. What is your name?"

He sounded friendly and interested, but I didn't have the time or patience for small talk. I had far too many pressing matters on my mind. "Carlos," I said, without slowing down.

"My sister donated puppies to a guide dog school, and I thought you might be interested in hearing about it," Jim said, walking backward in front of me.

"Mobility is not my problem," I said, trying to put him off. I was irritated now. It should have been obvious to this guy that I was getting around just fine. "I don't need a guide dog."

I knew he was just trying to be friendly, but I was afraid he was going to start asking me the typical questions sighted people often ask about blindness—how I got around, how I knew where I was, how I did things—those sorts of things. Normally, this wouldn't have bothered me. I want people to feel comfortable around me as a blind person, so, most of the time, I encourage people to ask questions, but I was feeling too stressed out lately with my personal problems to indulge people in this way.

I tried to walk faster and move to the left to go around him, but Jim was fast and stayed in front of me. He said, "So, tell me, what's your problem?" showing compassion about my situation.

I wanted to tell him it was none of his business, but I tried to think of a more polite way to end this exchange.

"Do you need food?" Jim persisted.

I shook my head.

"Do you need a place to stay?"

Again, I shook my head. This situation was becoming bizarre. His solicitude made me think of the priest. Who does this guy think he is to just go up to a complete stranger and ask such personal questions anyway?

Jim wouldn't give up. Still walking backward, he asked, "Immigration?"

He finally said something that caught my attention. Maybe this guy genuinely wanted to help. I decided to listen to what he had to say. After all, I still wanted to believe that God works to send people to us.

I stopped walking and nodded my head.

Excitedly, Jim said, "Tell me about it."

For a fleeting moment, I wondered whether Jim was an

immigration officer out to trap me in some way. I immediately dismissed that thought almost as soon as I had it. I was not doing anything wrong. I had a visa, and I was looking for a legal way to stay in the country. That's all. I made up my mind to tell Jim my story. I told him I needed a student visa to stay in the United States. I said I had all the necessary documentation for a student visa and had passed the English examination for international students; I had financial support for college expenses. All I needed was a sponsor. By then, we had reached the classroom.

Jim said, "I can be your sponsor!"

One of Jim's friends, another teacher, overheard our conversation and said, "Hey, Jim, are you sure you can do that? That's very serious stuff."

"Oh well. It's true that I don't have a lot of money. I'm only a city employee and a part-time teacher, but I have family, relatives, and friends all over the country. I'm sure some of them will help."

Jim sounded convinced. I could hardly believe what I was hearing. With the break nearly over, Jim had to get back to another class where he taught math. But since we were both done for the day at the same time, he offered to take me home so I could tell him more about the sponsorship.

For the next hour, I couldn't concentrate on anything my teacher said. My mind was spinning with hopeful speculations. As we walked to his car after class, and he drove to my apartment, I told him about the requirements for a student visa.

When we reached my apartment complex, Jim expressed anxious concern about the neighborhood.

"What do you mean?" I asked.

"There are some pretty rough-looking guys outside your buildings. A couple might be doing drugs. Another guy looks like he's passed out drunk."

Jim came in, and I explained to him as much as I could about the immigration process and what the responsibilities of a sponsor were. He still wanted to do it. I gave Jim the contact information for Joe Cordova and for the University of New Mexico (UNM) International Student Services office. As he left, he said he would pick me up from TVI the next afternoon. We would go together to meet with Joe Cordova and then to the UNM International Student Services office.

Jim acted as if this whole situation was no big deal. He showed no concern about the significance of the responsibility he was about to take on. I was happy but cautious too. Did he not fully understand the commitment he would be making? Jim hadn't talked to Joe or to the International Services office yet. I knew there was the very real possibility that Jim would change his mind once he knew what would be expected of him.

I nervously waited for Jim to pick me up outside TVI at the appointed time the next day. Jim didn't show up. Not good. Did Jim get cold feet? An hour later, I was still waiting. I thought maybe he had an accident, or an emergency came up. Maybe he was waiting at my apartment, but I didn't really believe it.

As I walked home, I couldn't help but feel bitter disappointment. I was now ready to give up. There was truly nothing more I could do. After everything I had been through, it had all come down to this. Totally defeated, I resigned myself to going back to Peru.

I didn't have much hope of finding work as an English teacher, either, not with so many other unemployed sighted people with better English skills looking for work. Peru had one of the highest unemployment rates in the world. A blind guy had almost no chance of finding meaningful work there.

I hoped Jim would call out to me as I reached the apartment complex parking lot, but that didn't happen. Inside my apartment, I started getting ready for dinner. I listened to the news on the radio, even though I really didn't feel like eating. I felt a sense of deep despair. It seemed so unfair—to have come so far only to have it end like this. Wallowing in sorrow, I heard a knock at the door.

I felt immediate alarm. No one ever came to visit since Philip left. I remembered what Jim said about the neighborhood looking dangerous.

Thinking that it might be a drug addict, I moved quietly to the door to listen for anything out of the ordinary. I couldn't pretend no one was home. The radio was on, so if someone was outside, they had to know I was in.

The knocking continued. "Carlos. Carlos, are you there? This is Jim."

Jim sounded scared. Was it because he was afraid of being in my building alone? I wasn't sure. I opened the door and told him to come in.

"Hi," he said and walked in. "Would you mind if I turned on the light?"

I hadn't realized it had gotten dark.

"I'm sorry I didn't pick you up earlier. When I left my day job, I realized I didn't have time to pick you up and still make it to both appointments."

I didn't know why Jim was here, but he certainly didn't owe me an explanation. If he didn't want to help me, that's fine. The decision was entirely up to him. But I wasn't interested in excuses, either. All he had to say was that he wasn't able to sponsor me after all. I knew how big of a commitment a sponsor would be making. It was a lot to ask.

"I called Joe to see if I could go and meet with him sooner than we had planned," Jim went on. "He was free, so I left work early. I had no way to let you know of the change in plans. Joe confirmed that the Commission for the Blind would pay for your tuition and books. We called the International Student Services office to find out exactly what they needed.

The director there knew who you were. She said that the Commission for the Blind needed to write a letter, signed by the director or deputy director, confirming the agency's coverage of college expenses. Joe wrote the letter and signed it. After that, I went straight to UNM before the International Student Services office closed. When I reached her office, the director had your file ready with your translated documents, your English examination results, and a copy of your medical visitor visa. She was very happy that you were able to find a sponsor. I signed a bunch of forms, including an affidavit."

As Jim talked, my spirits started to rise. Was he saying what I thought he was saying? I wanted to believe, but I didn't want to be set up for another disappointment. I concentrated on every word he said, powerful emotions welling up inside me. Perhaps that is why I remember his words so well.

Jim continued, "After I signed all the documents, she filled out these two forms and said that you need to sign them and bring them back to her tomorrow, so she can give you your student visa."

At first, I just looked at Jim, not knowing what to say. I was still trying to process everything he had been saying. It seemed too good to be true. Was this a practical joke? If so, I couldn't believe that this man could be so cruel. It had to be for real.

I smiled at him finally and said, "I don't know how to thank you, Jim. You don't know how much this means to me."

"You don't have to thank me. All I did was sign some forms. You are the one who will have to do the hard work!" Jim reached out to shake my left hand and pat my shoulder.

Jim showed me where to sign the forms and then said he needed to leave. "I need to go to write letters asking my family and friends for donations to help cover your living expenses." We shook hands again, and he left.

I woke the next morning with more positive energy and elevated spirits than I had had in a very long time. I had finally gotten a good night's sleep. The whole situation still seemed a bit unreal though, like a dream. Had my student visa really been approved? I ate my breakfast, singing happily, and then headed out for UNM International Student Services.

When I got there, the director was waiting for me. Still early, none of the other offices were open. She had my file with all of my documents ready to go.

"How are you doing?"

"Fantastic!" I said, smiling broadly. "I can't believe my good fortune. This is the answer to my prayers."

"You know, I don't think I have ever seen you smile. I am so happy for you."

I asked her for clarification about the F-1 and J-1 visas, particularly as it related to my ability to work. She confirmed what I already knew: For the J-1 visa I needed to maintain good grades and, after finishing my studies, I would have to return to Peru for at least two years. She added that, on the plus side, the J-1 visa would allow me to work up to twenty hours per week during the semester and unlimited hours during school breaks, whereas I wouldn't be able to work with an F-1 visa. She also said that a J-1 visa needed to be sponsored by a government entity. I thought she was reading my mind when she said, "The Commission for the Blind is a government agency, so I don't see why you can't have a J-1 visa."

"Thank you so very much," I said. My tense muscles relaxed immediately. I felt close to tears, and my voice was quivering with strong emotion. "This means a great deal to me."

Things could not have worked out better. Not only was my way clear for a college education in America, but also I would now be able to support myself at the same time. She presented me with the necessary forms to sign to certify the J-1 student visa, and our business was concluded. A sense of relief washed over me. She wished me well, and I left her office full of energy and eager to get on with my life.

Walking south on Yale Boulevard, I pictured the imposing Sandia Mountains to my left. The sunny day matched my disposition. I strode with purpose and determination. I felt unstoppable, ready to take on the next great challenge of my life—Cati's father. Now that I knew the path to college and career was open and secure, I had the confidence to talk to him about our relationship and plans for a future together.

• Chapter Twenty •

TAKING THE BULL BY THE HORNS

In early June, I applied to work for a summer work experience program for blind teenagers coordinated by the Commission for the Blind. I had Dick Davis's letter of recommendation and was confident I could teach Braille, cane travel, and some homemaking. Chris Boone, the program coordinator, offered me a job working the overnight shift. That gave me 45 hours per week (five hours more than other positions). I needed to earn enough money to live on, but I also needed to buy a plane ticket to Peru so I could talk to Cati's father.

Jim collected money for me, ten dollars here and there, and I appreciated his help, but I wanted to support myself. Still, I gratefully accepted what he offered. At that time in my life, it was a lot of money, and it helped pay the rent.

That February, I got my own phone and was able to call Cati through another aunt who lived nearby. Cati's aunt would go to her house under some pretext to let her know that I was on the phone. If we had agreed on the day and time for my next call, Cati would be waiting at her aunt's house.

Cati's father continued to oppose our relationship and was not happy when he found out we were still communicating. Although talking to Cati was wonderful, I didn't like hiding from her father, as if there were something wrong with our loving each other. Now that I had my student visa and was able to go back and forth to Peru, I told Cati I would come back to formally ask for her hand in marriage. Cati said she would let her father know that I was coming the first week in August to talk to him.

While on the plane, I imagined myself running up to Cati and hugging her like a scene in a movie. More than a year had passed since we last saw each other, and thoughts of our reunion made me almost desperate with anticipation. The plane couldn't go fast enough. In my mind's eye, I could see us holding hands, kissing each other, her soft, warm body close to mine.

I arrived at the Jorge Chavez airport in Lima the evening of August 7, but Cati wasn't there as I expected. What had gone wrong? Had something happened to her? I couldn't believe Cati had decided not to marry me after all. Our relationship was too strong for me to doubt what we meant to each other. I felt very dejected and confused.

Later, Cati told me that her father would not allow her to go out that late at night, especially to see me. When she told him I was coming to talk to him, he said we had nothing to discuss. As far as he was concerned, our relationship was a closed subject. I knew winning him over wouldn't be easy, but I didn't think he would refuse to meet with me. I was just as determined to speak with him as he was apparently deter-mined *not* to talk to me.

The next morning, I was on the phone talking to a friend

when there was a knock at the door. My sister went to answer it. When I heard Cati's voice, I immediately hung up the phone and stood up to meet her. She ran across the living room, and we fell into a fervent, passionate embrace. At first, neither of us said anything. I kissed her head, her forehead, her lips. We clung to each other in our frenzied, nearly all-consuming need to touch and be touched by each other, to know we were finally together in person.

After many long months, I was able to tell her how wonderful it was to be with her again. Cati hugged me hard and started to cry. She tried to talk, but her sobs made it hard to understand. Blinking back tears of my own, I tried and failed to find the words to express everything I was feeling. We were both completely overwhelmed by the raging emotions surging through us, pent-up for far too long. It had been sixteen months since I had last held Cati in my arms. I took her in, breathing in her scent as I kissed her tear-soaked face and patted her back.

My brothers and sisters applauded, reminding us that other people were there. Cati and I would have liked to be alone together, but there wasn't much time for that. We spent most of that day on the couch holding hands or with my left arm around her shoulders as friends and relatives kept coming by to visit.

In those moments when I could, I told Cati I was determined to talk to her father the next day, despite his opposition. That alarmed her. She feared it would not go well. Her father had been clear on the subject. He was dead set against our relationship.

The next morning, I was anxious but determined to face Mr. Alvarez and talk to him about the life Cati and I planned to have together. I wanted him to listen and understand. I had some reason to believe that he would. Mr. Alvarez and I were former policemen, and we policemen have a code of honor that includes mutual respect. Cati and I loved each other, and, just like any other couple, we wanted to be together.

The problem was, as far as Mr. Alvarez was concerned, because I was blind, he assumed, like most people in Peru, that I was incapable of supporting myself, let alone a wife and family. I knew Mr. Alvarez wanted someone with a career and a good job for his daughter, someone who would not have to depend on his wife financially.

As it got closer to the time to leave, I began to think about what could go wrong. The thought that a confrontation might go badly worried me. I steeled myself against such thoughts and tried to concentrate more on how I was going to prevail. Still, my palms were thick with sweat. My heart beat wildly.

The weather was cold and overcast when I finally got into a taxi that afternoon with my siblings Monica, Ernesto, and Gloria and made the trip to Rimac, a suburb next to Lima where Cati lived with her family. On the way over, lost in my own thoughts, I didn't say much. This should have been a happy occasion. In a "normal" relationship, it would have been. Asking a father for his daughter's hand in marriage was usually cause for celebration, with both sides of the family coming together in joyous merrymaking. I wanted that, but it would never happen unless I could convince Mr. Alvarez that I was good enough to marry his daughter. He was not a bad man. He loved his daughter and wanted only what was best for her. I knew that, because of my blindness, he did not see me as a suitable candidate for Cati's affection.

We finally arrived. My sisters and brother wished me good luck and stayed in the taxi. I rang the doorbell, and, after a couple minutes that felt like an eternity, Cati opened the door.

"My dad's out walking the dog, and he does not want to see you." Cati's voice encompassed the gloom I already felt.

I was momentarily taken aback, but I knew what Cati and I wanted and had waited for. He probably thought I would just leave if he wasn't home. I would not be so easily deterred.

"Alright. Then I will wait until he is back, no matter how long it takes." I tried to sound more sure of myself than I felt.

Actually, I had no idea if Mr. Alvarez would be coming back home that afternoon or not, but I was determined I would not leave until we talked. I didn't come all the way from America only to be turned away now.

As Cati let me into the living room, the tension in the air was palpable. Cati's brother, Mario, sounded friendly enough as he greeted me. Mrs. Alvarez was polite, if somewhat reserved. Her sister, Elvira, said nothing at all.

"Good afternoon." I nodded and sat down on the sofa next to Cati, facing the front door.

No one spoke. Cati squeezed my hand from time to time. The only sound was the tick-tock of the clock on the living room wall. We all waited to see what would happen next. The minutes crawled by. The silence hung like a shroud. The waiting seemed to take forever.

Finally, we heard Mr. Alvarez come through the front door with his dog, Lila, yapping excitedly. A half a minute later, he walked into the living room still talking to Lila in his usual authoritative voice. He stopped in mid-sentence when he saw me sitting on the couch with Cati. Only the clock on the wall and Lila's panting could be heard. I stood up to greet him.

"Good afternoon, Mr. Alvarez," I said with all the respect and confidence I could manage. He just stood there, saying nothing. I felt awkward.

"Good afternoon," he said finally. His tone was cordial, but then he started walking toward the stairs without another word. His response let us know, in no uncertain terms, that he was going to his room. He refused to speak to me.

I had sat back down next to Cati, but when I realized what he was doing, I stood up again. No one else moved as this drama between Mr. Alvarez and me played itself out. The suspense was excruciating. I had to take the next step.

"Mr. Alvarez," I began, "I came to talk to you about your daughter and me." To my relief, I sounded firm and determined—and thoroughly respectful.

"Young man, I never approved of this relationship and will not change my mind now. There is nothing to talk about!" He raised his voice as if he were addressing the cadets in military or police training.

"Why not?" I walked a fine line between not backing down while still trying to sound respectful.

Mr. Alvarez is not a man used to being challenged. Taking his time before answering, he lowered his voice and finally said, "Because of your condition."

It sounded like he did not want to hurt my feelings. Of course, I knew he was referring to my blindness, but I wanted him to say it. I wanted him to know I was comfortable talking about it. "What condition are you referring to?"

My boldness surprised him. I believe Mr. Alvarez did not think I could be so frank about my blindness. He hesitated before saying, "Because of the way you are."

"My height? The color of my skin? Or is it because I am blind?" I said, encouraging him to go on.

Cati's father, sounding exasperated by now, said, "Yes, it is because of your eye condition."

It was time to state my case. "Mr. Alvarez, I understand your concern. My mother is a widow, I have four sisters, and I may have a daughter someday. If I did not know much about the capabilities of blind people, I would probably be opposed to my future daughter, any of my sisters, or my widowed mother marrying a blind person, who would be unable to support himself and would be dependent on society and his family. On the other hand, I would want them to be happy, to marry the man who will make them happy. I would want them to marry someone who can support himself and provide for the family, someone who can be supportive in the most difficult times and bring stability. I have been living in America for over a year by myself. I live in an apartment by myself. I clean my apartment and do my laundry and my shopping. I have a part-time job, and I go to school full time. I am working for a state agency and also do some tutoring at the university and get paid as a teacher, around twelve dollars an hour. Let me be clear. I don't want to marry your daughter because I need someone to support me or to be my sighted guide. I look forward to marrying a woman who will make me happy and who is willing to face together the challenges that all married couples face." I stopped talking to give Mr. Alvarez time to absorb what I said.

Mr. Alvarez listened attentively. When he finally spoke, he raised his voice so no one would have any doubt about his position. "I am impressed, and I congratulate you on your courage, determination, and accomplishments. All the same, I don't agree with this relationship, and I do not give my permission for my daughter to marry you."

Cati was still holding my hand, and she started squeezing it more and more tightly. I think she was crying. Her family was still and silent, as if holding its collective breath. Even the dog stopped panting, so everyone could hear the ticking of the clock again. It was obvious that when Mr. Alvarez spoke, everybody listened. It had been the same with Papa in our home when I was growing up.

I stood as straight and tall as I could and squeezed Cati's hand before I spoke. "I don't believe I'm making myself clear. I did not come here to ask for your permission. I came here to let you know that Cati and I love each other, and we are going to get married. We would prefer that you accept that fact, because it will make everyone happier."

Mr. Alvarez watched his daughter crying. Leaning closer to me, he said, "Looking at my lovely daughter crying like that is breaking my heart and—"

"Mr. Alvarez," I interrupted, as gently as I could. "I am sorry, but this is not about feeling sorry for your daughter or me. I want you to understand that your daughter will not be my sighted guide and will not support me financially."

I thought I had pushed things too far. Cati's dad raised his voice louder still, making it clear that, in his house, his decisions were final. I felt Cati's hand relax in mine, as if to say, well, at least we tried our best.

But then he continued, "Very well then, young man! You have taken the bull by the horns! I am glad that my daughter fell in love with a man with your determination, your courage, and one who is able to confront me and make me see what you are made of. I accept your relationship, and I give my consent for my daughter and you to marry."

He walked toward me, and I stepped forward, extending my hand to shake his. Cati still held my arm. When Mr. Alvarez and I finished shaking hands, he hugged his daughter. Cati began to cry tears of happiness. Though she continued to clutch my left hand, I felt her body lean forward, and I assumed she had put her head on her dad's chest while he hugged her.

After that, Monica, Ernesto, and Gloria came in. This was the first time Cati's family had met any of mine. Mr. Alvarez was very happy to meet my younger siblings.

A couple of days after Mr. Alvarez gave his consent, Cati and I were married by the justice of the peace. Only close family members attended. The money I brought was not enough for a larger celebration or reception. We promised that next time I came back to Peru, we would have a big celebration, with friends and relatives included.

Cati was my wife now, and I could take her back to America, though not right away. We would have to navigate the immigration process first. It would be another year before she would be able to join me in Albuquerque.

I returned to the United States in a reflective mood. Overall, the past year and a half had gone better than I thought possible. With little money and next to no resources, I found a way to not only survive, but I was doing well. Cati and I were married, and I was about to start university-level classes in English. I knew I would have to find a job to support us. I was about to take on a whole different set of challenges, but given everything I had been through so far, I had every confidence that I would make it work.

• Chapter Twenty-One •

1992 NFB SCHOLARSHIP COMPETITION

The prospect of starting a new life as a college student in America thrilled and invigorated me. Things were finally working out in my favor. I realized I would continue to face new challenges, but I had the confidence to meet them head-on.

By the 1990s, almost all institutions of higher education in America had a special services office for students with disabilities. For blind students, the special services office coordinated support services such as readers, human note-takers, recorded textbooks, and test proctors. I was impressed and grateful that such a valuable resource was available to me—and others. In Peru, I had been completely on my own.

One of the most important lessons I learned from my fellow blind college students was that I needed to be in charge of my own education and not rely too heavily on special services. For example, I was advised not to use human note-takers. It would be better if I took my own notes. That way, they would be immediately available, and, because I wrote them myself, they would make more sense than notes taken by someone else.

I met Doris Chasey, Jim's mother, who became a great friend and an adopted grandmother. Cati and I named our daughter after her.

Doris was one of my earliest readers. I also had readers provided by UNM Special Services, mostly college students, but I never seemed to have enough. My first semester, I had four classes with textbooks and other required reading. I asked students in my classes if they would like to read for me. Not only would they be reading the books they were assigned to read anyway, but they would also be paid minimum wage for doing so. It worked pretty well for them, and I had control over who read for me too.

I was earning some money tutoring Spanish, but I could not work enough hours to support myself because of my class schedule and need for study time. Trying to coordinate the schedules of different readers was also time-consuming. My English had improved, but still it did not come as easily to me as Spanish, and that slowed me down. I slept only three to four hours at a time and used every spare minute reading the assignments.

The first semester was grueling. I thought it would never end. Though relieved when final exams came, I still felt apprehensive. I needed to maintain a B-plus average to keep my student visa. I worried that my grades would not be good enough. To find out my grades, I asked students passing by to look up my grade on a list posted on the wall outside each classroom. They were able to do so using my Social Security number. As it turned out, I got three As and one A minus. I was in seventh heaven! I knew in that moment I would be fine in college, especially if my English and my note-taking and studying skills kept improving. Then I could concentrate on finding more work. It was very important to me that I support myself and make my own way.

I was not sleeping well. Frequent headaches, strong pain in my remaining left eye, and persistent nightmares kept me awake. One recurring dream was particularly disturbing. It was the same one that had tormented me almost from the time right after I became blind. A shadowy figure would slip silently into my room, close the door, and come stand by my bed to choke me with gloved hands, as I lay in my bed awake but unable to do anything. Finally, one night, this nightmare was replaying in my mind again, but it was different this time. I understood that it was just a dream. It was not real. As the shadowy figure stood by my bed slipping gloves over his hands, I could feel my heart racing and my breath coming in short, rapid gasps. I focused on controlling my heartbeat and breathing. As the cold fingers encircled my throat, I thought, "You are not real. I am not afraid. Damn you."

I woke up. No one was there. Everything was still and quiet. The nightmare had been with me for about five years, but that was the last time I experienced it. I never had it again. Nightmares reflect our fears and vulnerabilities. The opposite is also true. Pleasant dreams reflect our sense of personal security and being in control. I resolved then to be as positive as I could every day and focus on the opportunities before me.

As a blind person, it was important for me to stay connected to successful blind people. I continued to attend NFB local chapter meetings, state and national conventions, and seminars for blind students. With the information and encouragement I received, I did well in school and continued to earn As.

That first summer after starting college, Chris Boone offered me a job again working with blind students. Things were going well. In August 1991, Cati joined me in Albuquerque. Doris Chasey held a party for us, and our circle of friends quickly expanded.

Having the woman I loved at my side brought joy and peace to my life. Cati and I moved to a new apartment on Colombia Street, just a few blocks from the main entrance to the campus. Finally, we no longer had to maintain a long-distance relationship over the phone. Cati would be there anytime I needed someone to talk to. It had taken a long time, but Cati and I were together at last. Whatever challenges and difficulties lay ahead, I would not be alone. Cati and I would face the future together. We would learn that celebrations, dreams, disappointments, arguments, and reconciliations are the journey of marriage.

The idea of working for the government and making a positive difference in people's lives always appealed to me. For that reason, I decided to study political science and eventually attend law school. In Peru, most of the executives of governmental agencies, including public officials and congressmen, were lawyers.

I had been active in the NFB for some time when, in March 1992, I applied for a scholarship. Every July, the federation presents scholarships at the national convention. I wasn't sure that my application would be given serious consideration since I had only been in the US for a short time, so it came with some surprise when I got word that I was one of twenty-six finalists to be invited to the NFB national convention in Charlotte, North Carolina. As a scholarship finalist, all of my expenses were paid. About 2,700 blind people from all over the nation and around the world attended the convention, making it the largest gathering of blind people in the world. We stayed in four different five-star hotels surrounding the Charlotte Convention Center.

The scholarship application process was rigorous. Applicants submitted academic transcripts, three recommendation letters, and an essay introducing ourselves and describing our leadership potential. Approximately 600 blind students applied for the NFB scholarships that year.

The scholarship finalists represented a variety of public and private universities, including some of the nation's most prestigious institutions.

A mandatory meeting for the finalists was held on the first day of the convention. We heard from Dr. Marc Maurer, NFB president; Dr. Kenneth Jernigan, president emeritus; and members of the scholarship committee, all of whom were accomplished blind leaders from across the country.

Dr. Jernigan offered the wisdom of his experience. He described his life growing up in rural Tennessee before there was an NFB. He talked about how many of the opportunities we now take for granted are the direct result of the federation and its work. He said that the future was ours to claim if we wanted it. We could not wait for society to create opportunities for us; we had to forge them for ourselves. I considered it a great honor to hear from such an articulate and inspirational leader and teacher.

President Maurer shared his experiences as a blind university student, emphasizing that just because we were capable students, did not necessarily mean we would be strong leaders. He said that the purpose of the scholarship program was to encourage and support us, but we, in turn, had an obligation to encourage and support others. I observed that Dr. Jernigan and Dr. Maurer have intellectual fire power.

Next, the members of the scholarship committee introduced themselves. Their credentials and achievements were quite impressive. The group included successful public officials, business people, lawyers, and university professors—who were all there to teach us and to help us find our place in the federation family. The message was simple. When one blind person is successful, all blind people benefit; when one blind person faces discrimination, we all suffer discrimination.

When it was our turn to introduce ourselves, we all tried to put our best foot forward. As I listened to the other finalists introduce themselves, I felt humbled. Some of them attended prestigious universities, and some were enrolled in master's or doctoral programs. I felt out of place and was sure that I had no chance of getting a top scholarship. Still, I was glad just to be here at all, to meet so many great people, and to attend the convention with all expenses paid.

President Maurer told us that the final decision about who would receive the top scholarships would be made during the week based on an assessment of our leadership potential. He said that, based on our applications, they were satisfied that we were accomplished students. The question was whether or not we were willing and able to make the world a better place for blind people.

His words moved me. I felt like he was talking directly to me! Not only was I willing to help others, but also it was what I wanted to do.

During the week, I asked many questions. I wanted to understand the federation and how its philosophy could be put into day-to-day practice. When I thought I could contribute, I offered my ideas, but I was not always reserved and serious. I have a sense of humor and joked when I thought it was appropriate. Also, I sold as many raffle tickets and Peruvian earrings as I could to raise funds for the New Mexico Association of Blind Students.

My three suits and ties came from The Salvation Army at one dollar each. I wanted to look presentable and thought that lack of money was no excuse for dressing poorly. Dressing as professionally as I could showed respect for the organization that had done so much to advance opportunities for blind people.

The scholarship finalists were assigned mentors for each

day of the convention. I went to meetings with my mentors, including the general sessions. I discussed the presentations with them and talked about what we could do to advance the cause of the federation. The mentors took notes, and that made me nervous. I felt like I was being scrutinized, and I suppose I was.

Throughout the week, my mentors introduced me to other federation leaders. All received me warmly and offered to help with anything I might need. They answered my questions patiently and seriously, even though, looking back, I'm sure many of my queries were basic and naive. I met attorneys, business owners, rehabilitation and mental health counselors, teachers, and government officials. I was thrilled and honored to meet so many distinguished blind people.

During the week, I met Avraham "Rami" Rabby, the first blind US Foreign Service officer. In 1988, the State Department denied Rami's Foreign Service application based on his blindness. Predictably, the State Department cited "safety" and "national security considerations," even though he had already passed three written and two oral entrance examinations.

Rami's qualifications were impeccable. He had a degree from Jesus College at Oxford University and a master's of business administration from the University of Chicago. He was fluent in English, French, Spanish, and Hebrew. But Rami was not just qualified, he was a federationist. The federation took his case before Congress and the media until the State Department was forced to reverse its position. I was studying international political science, so I had many questions for Rami.

The highlight of the week was the convention banquet. The banquet is a time of celebration and a time of reflection. President Maurer delivered an address entitled, "The Mysterious Ten Percent." I hung on his every word. President Maurer explained that the discrimination we face is not the result of conscious, deliberate thought, but just the opposite—a lack of thought and reflection.

"One of the accepted doctrines throughout history has been that it is essential to be able-bodied to be productive. The blind are not in this group. Hence, we are told that we have very limited capacity . . . . So completely fixed is this idea that further examination is presumed by many to be irrelevant."

President Maurer continued, "Our own experience refutes that commonly held belief. Thousands of us have demonstrated that we are able to handle the ordinary job in the ordinary place of business, and (as with the sighted) some blind people demonstrate extraordinary ability and make remarkable contributions. Nevertheless, the notion of the incapacity of the blind remains firmly embedded in the thinking of millions."

President Maurer did not believe that second-class status was impossible to change. He pointed to our progress over the years as proof that together we have and will continue to change the public perception of the blind as incapable.

He ended his address with a call to action. "If we cannot muster the courage, sustain the dream, or maintain the nerve, the loss will be unimaginable. But, of course, we will not fail. We have one another, and nobody . . . can prevent us from going the rest of the way toward freedom. We believe in one another; we have faith in the ability of our blind brothers and sisters; and we will share the burden that must be borne to bring true independence to the blind."

The scholarship presentation followed President Maurer's address. The federation would award twenty-six scholarships, ranging from $2,000 to $10,000. There were twelve scholarships in the amount of $2,000, nine for $2,500, one for $3,000, three for $4,000, and one for $10,000. The winner of the $10,000 Ezra Davis Memorial Scholarship would be invited to address the banquet attendees.

Peggy Pinder (now Elliot), a Yale Law School graduate, NFB second vice president, and the scholarship committee chairperson, took the microphone and began speaking. That was the signal for the scholarship finalists to make their way to the platform. I was nervous as Peggy described each of the scholarships. The $2,000 winners would be called first, and the winner of the $10,000 top scholarship would be called last.

When I reached the platform, I looked for the beginning of the line, thinking that I would be one of the first ones called. A volunteer helped us line up in order. When I tried to step forward, he asked me to move back and placed another student in front of me. That happened several times. Peggy finished announcing all the $2,000 winners. I became a bit uneasy. I really did not think that I would be seriously considered for anything other than one of the smaller scholarships. Was there some kind of mistake?

Then I heard Fred Schroeder's voice nearby, "Hmmm, your name wasn't called. I wonder what's going on?"

He sounded like he was serious. Did he really think something was wrong? I didn't know. It made me nervous. Peggy called a few more names.

"You still haven't been called," Fred said. "You don't suppose they forgot you, do you, my friend?"

This time, I could tell that Fred was enjoying himself. He was teasing me, but why? This was no time to be funny. This was no joke. I was wound up too tight to appreciate the humor.

Peggy called another name, and Fred said, "My friend, why haven't you been called?"

I ignored Fred and tried to concentrate on what Peggy was saying, but I was actually starting to panic. I was sure by now that something was definitely not right. The person organizing the line of scholarship winners kept moving me back. Had I been disqualified?

Just when I thought I couldn't be more nervous, Fred said, "I think they forgot to call you."

I was ready to snap.

Then he said, "My friend, there is no one behind you."

I turned to check with my cane to find out if what he had said were true. Just then, Peggy said, "The winner of the $10,000 Ezra Davis Memorial Scholarship is . . ." The ballroom became quiet, filled with anticipation, "Carlos Serván of New Mexico!"

Fred touched my shoulder and said, "Congratulations, my friend."

I was overcome with emotion. My mind went blank. I could not think of a single thing to say. I needed to get myself together. I could not believe it! My God! I was going to get $10,000?! I forced myself to focus. Remember, you have to give a speech. I tried to concentrate on Peggy's words:

"Carlos will be a senior in the fall at the University of New Mexico, where he is earning a bachelor's degree in political science and Latin American studies, but that tells you very little about Carlos. He intends to be a lawyer, either in international business or in civil rights, but that doesn't tell you much about Carlos, either. He is originally from Peru. After graduating from high school and while studying some college courses, Carlos joined Peru's special military forces, which combat guerrillas and conduct counter-terrorism activities. In a terrorist attack several years ago, Carlos lost his eyesight and one hand.

"He came to the United States less than two years ago to receive the more sophisticated medical treatment he needed, and he found other things in addition. Not speaking one word of English when he came, he found a new language. He also found our kind of freedom, and he found a new way of life in the National Federation of the Blind.

"Practically since he came into the States, he has served as the president of the student division of the National Federation of the Blind of New Mexico. If you have been around this convention at all, you have bought a raffle ticket from Carlos Serván."

As I approached the podium, I still didn't know what I could say to express my gratitude to everyone who had helped me. As I crossed the platform, Dr. Jernigan shook my hand and congratulated me. It was wonderful. It was the first time I had been so close to him. Then President Maurer shook my hand. I felt honored to be in the presence of these two great leaders. I heard people chanting, "Speech! Speech!"

I thought of my mother who suffered—maybe more than I did—when I lost my eyesight. I thought of my humble roots in Peru, my poor neighborhood, the jobs I had as a teenager, and getting into the police academy. I thought about the struggles I faced when I arrived in the United States and all my sleepless nights studying.

The chanting stopped, and the audience waited to hear me speak. The hall was silent as I stepped to the microphone. Powerful emotions washed over me, but I spoke with all the calm I could manage.

"Thank you, federationists. First of all, I would like to thank the members of the scholarship committee and its chairman, Peggy Pinder. Let me try to tell you a little bit about how I feel and how I love this federation. All this week, I have felt that the hotels were full of energy, and I feel energized to be a part of this group, this National Federation of the Blind.

"Last Sunday, President Maurer talked to us, the scholarship members, and he mentioned how important it is to keep ourselves busy. After the banquet speech tonight, let me tell you, President Maurer, that I promise you—and not only you, but all the federation, because I'm part of the federation—that I am going to be very busy serving blind people in this country and all over the world. I will be busy also to learn and teach the 10 percent that you were talking about.

"I would also like, with your permission, to thank two women. One is Eileen Rivera. When I came to Maryland, and the doctors told me that I wouldn't see again, I wanted to find out something about blindness. Eileen asked me, 'What is your philosophy about blindness?'

"I answered her, 'I think a blind person can do whatever he wants to do. All he needs is opportunity and training.'

"She told me, 'That's our philosophy.'

"I said to her, 'Who is this *our?* Who is *us?*' So she told me about the federation, and I attended my first national convention in 1989, a month after I had come to this country. Let me tell you the truth. I was a little skeptical of the things she told me about many blindness professionals. However, as Mr. Maurer mentioned also, we have learned little by little. And we won't ever forget what the federation is doing for us.

"I went to the orientation center at Alamogordo, and I was busy learning English and basic skills. I used to tell the administrator, Mr. Davis, that I would like to be a lawyer if I could. He never doubted me; he just told me, 'Yes, you will.' That is the federation. Nobody in the federation ever told me, 'Maybe.' They always told me, 'Yes, you will.'

"I also want to thank my wife for her support. This is her first convention. In very hard times, especially when we had my younger brother and sister living with us, studying full time, working, she was there all the time. She is a federationist. She understands our philosophy of blindness.

"To end, I would like to emphasize my thankfulness to Dr. Jernigan. I have been listening to and reading his speeches. Dr. Jernigan, you have kept the federation in the right way. The federation is changing the lives of many blind people in America. Dr. Jernigan, you will continue to change the lives of many, and I am going to repeat something that you have said in many of your speeches: 'We won't ever again settle for being second-class citizens.' Thank you."

The banquet room exploded with applause. After the banquet, I looked for Joe Cordova to thank him for all his support and guidance. He was delighted that a student from New Mexico (where he was the affiliate president) had won the top scholarship. Joe was the first one to meet me when I came to Albuquerque, and he was my first role model and mentor. Several more friends extended their congratulations and well wishes. Then, Cati and I went off to celebrate by ourselves.

On the way back to Albuquerque after the convention, I thought about all the speeches I had heard and all the wonderful people I had met. I especially appreciated the convention, not only because my command of English had improved but also because, as a scholarship winner, I had mentors to answer my many questions and to help me process what I was hearing. The convention would have been uplifting for any blind person. I was so fortunate and grateful to be adopted by this great country and meet the wonderful leaders working to improve the lives of blind people. That is when I came truly to believe that blind people can live a full, meaningful life—the life we want. I thus concluded:

We do not see colors, but we paint and decorate our lives in other ways.

We do not have eyesight to see the things around us, but we have the vision to shape our future.

We cannot drive a car, but we have the driving force to change our destiny.

We cannot see the faces of our loved ones, but we can feel their love filling our lives with joy.

We cannot see the smiles of our children, but we know what we need to do to make them happy.

We do not see who is on the other side of the street, but we know how to cross the road to continue the journey toward first-class status.

We cannot see the sunrise or the sunset, but we have inner passion igniting our souls with purpose, making us unstoppable.

Receiving the top scholarship helped me become known by other blind leaders across the country. The $10,000 was wonderful (most students need cash); however, as the scholarship chairperson and President Maurer mentioned several times, I gained the most from the trust, help, and love I received from the federation. The federation embodied triumph over adversity. As I thought about it, I realized they did not help me just because I was blind and needed money. The federation helped as many blind people as possible. The scholarship signified that they had placed their trust in me, and they had confidence that I would do whatever I could to pass on to others the help and encouragement I had received. It seemed to me that my two worlds had come together— growing up in Peru and now living in America.

Other wonderful news happened that year. Benedicto Jimenez, a lieutenant colonel now, created a special intelligence group to capture leaders of the terrorists in Peru. On September 12, 1992, this special group headed by him, captured the head of Shining Path, Abimael Guzmán. I remember meeting him at the detective academy. I learned later that year that several of my friends from the detective academy were involved in this historic event. The future for Peru was now looking better.

The National Federation of the Blind of New Mexico (NFBNM) state convention was held in April 1993. Dr. Maurer was the national representative. After the banquet, I was invited to the presidential suite. Dr. Maurer, Fred Schroeder, Joe Cordova, and several other federation leaders were there, talking about the convention.

At one point, Dr. Maurer said, "Carlos, you have done a great job since coming to America. We are proud of you."

"I was lucky, Dr. Maurer, to find the NFB and leaders like all of you in this room," I said, not sure how to respond even though his praise felt very welcome.

"Carlos," he said, "do you know the definition of luck?" Dr. Maurer was a man who always took the opportunity to teach others. It was one of the things I admired about the man, even if it made me nervous sometimes.

"Well," I said cautiously, "luck is when something good happens to you, something unexpected and good."

He considered that for a moment, and I thought he must have been satisfied with my answer. Then he said, "Carlos, the Roman philosopher Seneca once said, 'Luck is what happens when preparation meets opportunity.' Never forget it!"

"What are your plans in the mid and long term?" he asked then.

"Well, Dr. Maurer, I have given it a great deal of thought, and I would eventually like to be the president of an NFB state affiliate and, later, the director of a state agency for the blind."

"That is very ambitious, but with luck, you will."

As usual, I came away feeling enriched after talking to Mr. Mauer.

I graduated from UMN with honors in May 1993. I had letters of recommendation for law school. However, I did not do well on the Law School Admission Test (LSAT). I was disappointed. Fred Schroeder and I discussed the problem. Even though I could read textbooks and understand most of the lectures, English was not my first language. When I took the LSAT, I did not have time to look up the definitions of the words I didn't know. In addition, the LSAT was designed for Americans and used expressions I did not understand.

One evening, Fred called and said that he wanted to talk to the administrators at UNM Law School to explain my situation. I was not sure what could be done, but I agreed to go with him. Fred was articulate as he reviewed my accomplishments in the few years I had been in America. He also told them that his background was in education and that he had observed me and trusted my capacity to do well in law school. He ended by telling them to look more at my grades, track record, and the letters of recommendation from my professors.

A couple of weeks later, I received a letter from the UNM Law School Admissions Office, stating that I did not do well on the LSAT, but that a determination regarding my admission had been deferred until I completed an eight-week summer class. The class included several Hispanic applicants, one African American, several Native Americans, and one blind guy (me)—all total around thirty students from diverse and minority backgrounds. Law professors conducted the intense class. We all studied hard, and, at the end of the course, we were all accepted.

As I finished my first year of law school, I wondered what I would do in Peru with an American law degree if I could not obtain US residency. My mother had applied for residency for me under her visa, but the Immigration and Naturalization Service's waiting list was very long—another five or six years at least. In addition, I wanted to be an administrator, but law school did not include public administration.

Unsure of my options, I did some research and learned about dual graduate degrees, or the equivalent of two graduate programs together. Law school takes three years and graduate degrees take two years. If I did a dual degree, I could finish in four years, but I would have to study even harder. Because I was on the dean's list, because I believed in my abilities and drive, and because I believed the encouragement of those around me, I decided to add a master's in public administration to my law degree.

Chapter Twenty-Two

STEP

Fred Schroeder, the director of the commission, was born in Peru, but he was adopted at a young age and grew up in America. He did not speak Spanish. Since Fred and I were both from Peru, I wanted to invite him to our apartment for dinner. A perfect opportunity presented itself at a monthly NFB Albuquerque chapter meeting. At the end of each meeting, a member brought something to be auctioned off to raise money. At one such meeting in the spring of 1992, I offered a Peruvian dinner, and Fred Schroeder was the highest bidder.

Fred came over with his wife, Cathy. We had a fine meal of salad and aji de gallina—shredded chicken cooked with a creamy cheese salsa with Peruvian chili and spices. We talked about the similarities and differences between the Peruvian and New Mexican cultures. We also drank a fine red wine I brought back from Peru. We talked about the philosophy of the NFB and how much work still remained to be done. Fred mentioned the STEP (Summer Training and Employment Program) and its significance. He said that very few blind teenagers have the same kind of job opportunities sighted kids have. He also said that blind people have the highest unemployment rate in society—approximately 70 percent—because of lack of training and opportunity.

"Carlos, Louisiana and New Mexico are the first states to establish summer work programs for blind teenagers," Fred said. "In Louisiana, the NFB affiliate operates a training center similar to the Orientation Center for the Blind in New Mexico. They coordinate a summer work program for blind youth very much like our STEP program."

The STEP program had been on my mind a lot lately. Chris Boone had coordinated the program for the past couple of years, but I heard that she was taking time off this summer to take care of her young children. I was hoping to work in STEP again, but I worried that the new coordinator might not hire me.

"Fred, do you know if Chris Boone is going to run the STEP program again this year?"

"I'm not sure. Chris told me she needed to take time off for her new baby, and I don't know if she will be available."

"Would you let me know as soon as possible if Chris is going to coordinate the program this summer and, if not, who the new coordinator will be?"

I was leaning on Fred, I knew, but it was important for me to know so I could plan accordingly. I wanted to introduce myself to the new coordinator as soon as possible if it came to that.

"Sure. As a matter of fact, we are running short on time, so we will be making a decision very soon."

We had another glass of wine and talked more about the Spanish and English languages and about the different

Spanish words used in Peru, Spain, Mexico, and America. For instance, in Peru and Spain, a tortilla is an omelet. In Mexico and America, a tortilla is a thin, round, flat bread. You can imagine my confusion when I was offered a tortilla in Albuquerque. I expected an omelet and had asked for a fork to eat it with, but I was given a flat, round piece of bread instead.

After a satisfying dinner, Fred promised to call as soon as he had the name of the new STEP coordinator.

One night a couple of weeks later, I was studying for my midterm examinations, writing papers, and trying to get ahead in my reading assignments, when the phone rang. I answered and heard Fred's booming voice on the other end.

We exchanged greetings before he got right to the point. "Carlos. Remember I told you I would call when I knew who would be running the STEP program this summer?"

"Yes. Is Chris back to work, or do you have someone new?"

"No, no. Chris is still on leave of absence, but I found someone new."

He paused, so I asked, "Can you tell me who it is?"

"Yes, it's you."

I was speechless. I must have misunderstood what he meant or heard him incorrectly.

After a moment, I asked again, "Who?"

"You, my friend. You have very good references, and I would like you to run the STEP program this summer. Are you interested?" Fred said, sounding amused.

This time, without hesitation, I answered, "Yes. Yes, of course!"

Fred's tone became more businesslike. "Alright, Carlos, you need to fill out an application as soon as possible. You should plan on starting in the next few weeks. Joe Cordova will be your supervisor and will let you know what we need to do to get ready for summer. Do you have any questions?"

I had many, many questions, but kept them to myself. I

wanted to ask who the references were and what they had said. Why me and not someone else? What made them sure I can do the job? My English was still rough, and I have a heavy accent. Would the students, parents, and employers understand me? But I told Fred I had no questions.

"Okay, Carlos, that's great. I'll talk with you soon. And, hey, congratulations."

After hanging up, I just stood there by the phone for a while, still taking it all in. Though thrilled to have such a great job, I was also scared I would not do well. I didn't want to disappoint Fred and Joe.

"Are you okay?" Cati's question snapped me out of my self-absorption.

"Yes, I am. Fred just offered me the STEP program coordinator position."

"You don't want it? You don't look happy." Cati lightly touched my arm.

"Oh, no, I really want the job, but I'm afraid that I might not do well and may not live up to Fred's expectations."

"Fred is a very smart man and wants the Commission for the Blind to provide good services. If he didn't think you could do the job, he wouldn't have asked you."

Cati's confidence in me sealed the deal, and I accepted the position. I had so much to do. My mind raced. I started thinking about how I would find jobs for the blind students and how I would deal with employers who were reluctant to hire blind teenagers. I brainstormed ways to train the students at their job locations, deal with discipline problems, find and hire the right staff, and so on. The new and extraordinary challenge of coordinating the STEP program provided me with an amazing opportunity. The job was complicated and the expectations for me were high, but it was also a chance to prove to myself that I could do a good job and live up to the faith others had placed in me.

Few employers, including state and city government employers, realize the capabilities of blind youth. For this reason, the New Mexico Commission for the Blind established a work experience program for blind youth known as the Summer Training and Employment Program (STEP). The STEP program brought blind high school students to Albuquerque for the summer and placed them in jobs based on their individual interests and capabilities.

The Commission for the Blind staff worked with local employers to identify summer jobs for the blind STEP program participants. The employers did not pay the wages, but they were expected to give the students real work and hold them to the same standards expected of all employees. The Job Training Partnership Act, a federal program, paid the students' wages.

Because I imagined many blind students were not aware of the STEP program, as the new program coordinator, I made outreach a priority. I sent applications to all the public schools in the state, including the New Mexico School for the Visually Handicapped (now the New Mexico School for the Blind and Visually Impaired).

Next, I needed jobs for the blind students. I got a list of state and local government agencies and nonprofit organizations with offices in Albuquerque. I sent each government and private agency a letter emphasizing the importance of blind youth having summer jobs. I stressed that, with the Commission for the Blind's training and support, blind students could work successfully and just needed the opportunity to show what they could do.

We recruited blind high school students from across the state. They were housed at the University of New Mexico (UNM) dormitories in Albuquerque. The idea of working and earning some money over the summer attracted students, but the STEP program offered more than a summer job. In addition to work, the blind students learned important independent living skills, including how to take public transportation to and from their jobs.

Sighted teenagers go to summer camps, participate in sports, find jobs, and so on, but most blind teenagers do not. I was determined to do whatever I could to broaden their life experiences, as the Commission for the Blind had done for me. The summer would be busy, but I was used to hard work and liked the challenge, especially knowing that the Commission's director and deputy director supported me. I knew the students needed training, encouragement, and people who cared about and believed in them. I also knew that without programs like STEP, most of them had nothing to do over the summer. Being idle at home only served to reinforce their sense of inadequacy and dependency.

Today, more and more blind people, including blind youth, have disabilities in addition to blindness. That year, twenty-one high school age students applied for the STEP program. Of the twenty-one, eleven had additional disabilities. I talked to Fred and Joe, and we agreed to accept all of them. We knew that the students who had additional disabilities needed the program as much as, if not more, than the students who were just blind.

Joe said we needed to take into account the impact of multiple disabilities without compromising our expectations. He recommended we hire job coaches to work with them. The job coaches provided one-on-one training specific to the individual's other disabilities to assist them in learning and performing their job duties effectively and independently. After analyzing the job duties, they developed individual training plans. The goal was for the students to gradually work more and more independently until the job coaches were no longer needed.

We had students who, in addition to their blindness, also

had traumatic brain injuries, cerebral palsy, Down syndrome, hemiplegia, paraplegia, intellectual and cognitive disabilities, deafness, or a combination of disabilities. Regardless of their disabilities, we maintained an expectation of independence. In addition to job coaches, we also hired teachers to work with the students in the dorm on the activities of daily living. The students knew that once they learned the skills necessary to function independently, both the job coaches and dorm teachers would transition out.

As I mentioned earlier, there are two approaches to training for the blind: the traditional medical model and the Structured Discovery method. The public schools and the school for the blind used the traditional medical model, while the Commission for the Blind used the Structured Discovery method. Structured Discovery emphasizes confidence building and a problem-solving approach. It does not include old, traditional concepts like "learn to accept your limitations" that only discourage people from exploring their potential. What young blind people need is the confidence to try. Structured Discovery encourages individuals to develop their interests and seek out the skills that enable them to follow their dreams.

Before the program began, I met with the staff to go over procedures and make sure we all understood our roles. I began the staff training by saying, "You are here only if you believe in the capability of blind people and you are willing to use your energy, talent, and imagination to elevate the students' expectations. We must demonstrate that we care about them, believe in them, and want them to be successful—not just in the STEP program, but for their entire lives."

At the student orientation, I told the participants, "We, the blind, are disadvantaged less by our blindness and more by society's low expectations of us. The general public, employers, and professionals, including many teachers and reha- bilitation counselors, do not believe that we can be truly independent and productive. Also, we must recognize that we are part of society and often accept low expectations without question. The STEP program will strengthen your self-confidence and allow you to challenge those low expectations. You will find that you can do your jobs well and can take care of your rooms, do your own laundry, and manage your own money. We want you to believe in yourselves, and we will be there for you. Together we will find solutions to any problems you face.

"The Commission staff will teach you what you need to know. They will teach you how to clean your dorm rooms, how to carry your own cafeteria trays, how to get to the bus stop, how to do your jobs, and how to get back using public transportation after work. I want you to do your best, and we will be there to support you every step along the way. We have high expectations for you, and we believe in you.

"All of you will go to bed on time and follow the rules. You are expected to get up on your own, go to breakfast, and get to work on time. We will pay for all of your meals for the first week, but after you get your first paycheck, you will have to set aside money for food for the weekends. During the week, we will provide breakfast and lunch in the cafeteria, but not on weekends. You will have to go to restaurants and buy your meals, and no one is allowed to borrow or lend money.

"We will have group activities several evenings during the week and during the day on weekends. Successful blind people will talk to you and share their experiences and advice. Whenever possible, you will be expected to use public transportation. Recreational activities will include going to the mall, bowling, rock climbing, water rafting, zip lining, horseback riding, outdoor cooking on a charcoal grill, and more. We will teach you what you need to know, and throughout the summer, we will encourage and support one another."

The recreational activities were new to the program this

year, and some of the students objected to the planned activities, arguing that they were not safe. We explained that we would teach them what they needed to know. Structured Discovery, we assured them, is not a "throw them in the deep end of the pool, and they'll learn to swim" approach. Structured Discovery teaches nonvisual ways to function independently. As an individual's skills level increases, they are able to take on more and more challenging activities. We told the students that they would not be the only ones participating in the activities; blind staff would participate right along with them. We also told them that we would not ask them to do anything we were not willing to do ourselves.

The students who had multiple disabilities were the ones who were best at following the rules and showed the most determination when participating in the planned activities. Since the students who had multiple disabilities had not been expected to do much at home or at school, they were eager to try out new things and prove to themselves that they could be independent and successful. Their positive attitudes encouraged the other students to try harder and to participate actively, too.

I confess that at times I had doubts about the ability of some of the students with multiple disabilities to be independent. However, I wanted them to be challenged and pushed out of their comfort zone. I wanted them to become as independent as possible. I wanted them to be successful. Their needs were different from some of the other students, but we did not give up on them. Instead, we modified our approach and tried different strategies to help them succeed.

We had high expectations for all the STEP participants. All the students were expected to carry their own trays in the cafeteria, go through the food line independently, carry their own trays to the table, and empty the trash when they finished eating. They were expected to make their beds each morning before they left for work, keep their rooms clean, and do their own laundry. The students also made their own bag lunch each morning, and they went to restaurants for their meals on the weekends. In the beginning, some of the students complained that we were expecting too much. But as they saw the blind staff doing everything they were asked to do, the complaints stopped. They became motivated and adjusted to function independently. Seeing how the students with multiple disabilities did everything they were expected to do without complaint motivated them to do more for themselves.

The participants learned that we had high expectations for them and that the program staff would be firm—not to punish them, but because we cared about them and believed in them. All the participants learned a great deal during the summer. Some learned more than others, but all gained skills and confidence that prepared them to take on new challenges. At the graduation ceremony, with their parents and employers present, I said, "Remember to be independent at home and at school. Take out your own garbage, make your own beds, clean your rooms, carry your own trays in the cafeteria, and use your canes at all times. And never forget that it is okay to be blind." I hoped the students felt the same pride in themselves and their abilities and accomplishments as I did.

That fall, I continued to work part-time for the Commission for the Blind. About a month after the STEP program had ended, I got a call from an irate student named Michelle. "Why didn't you send me an application for the STEP program? I was at home all summer doing nothing!"

Confused, I asked her what school she attended and how old she was. I had the list of the schools that had received the applications, so I knew that at least I could fix the problem next year. She told me that she was from the School for the Blind in Alamogordo. I politely told her that 30 applications had been sent to the school and ten had been returned. I did not mention it to Michelle, but I had asked to go to the school to talk with the students about the program, but the school administration would not allow it. Michelle insisted that she never got an application. I told her to give me her mailing address and her parents' number and I would make sure that an application was sent to her next year. She did. She also asked me to send several applications to her at the school. Michelle and the other disgruntled blind students who had not been told about the STEP program complained to the school's administration. It became quite a scandal.

The following summer, I received thirty-eight applications, including Michelle's. I accepted all thirty-eight students. As with the prior year, around half of the students had other disabilities in addition to blindness. When the program began that summer, I asked Michelle, "How did you learn about STEP, and why were you so upset?" I wanted to know this to find out if I had done something wrong or had failed to do something, so I could fix the problem.

"Well, Carlos, when we got back from the summer break, we saw a big change in some of the students."

"What do you mean by 'a big change'?"

"Well, we saw several students walking on their own, using their canes—different from the ones we have, carrying their trays, and dropping off their garbage after they ate. Not only that, but most of them were students with multiple disabilities. We noticed a big difference in their confidence and independence, so we asked them where and how they learned all of that. They told us that they went to the STEP program with Carlos and that they also worked and got paid. We could not believe it! Learning independent living skills and working and getting paid! We were not told that we could get jobs or learn to be independent. A lot of us were at home doing nothing, arguing with our parents, and sitting around bored for three long months."

Michelle's enthusiasm made me realize that the best advertising any program can have is to make a difference in people's lives. That is what STEP was all about. We tried to provide good training based on high expectations. The difference we made showed in the participants, and they shared their experiences with others. Their testimonies were more than just words. The difference in their lives had become evident to everyone around them. We were not just there to teach skills. We used the skills to support high expectations, and we used the high expectations to show the students that we cared about them and wanted them to have fulfilling lives. We tried to walk the extra mile with each and every student. And I believe our faith in them made a difference.

The following year, I received forty-six applications. The STEP program was growing. I needed to work with DOL, Department of Labor, to secure enough slots to pay the students. I also needed to line up enough employers for everyone to have a job. But it was not enough just to find a warm seat for the students and call it a job. We needed employers who would treat the students as real employees, with the same expectations they had for their sighted staff.

Just as I was ready to begin hiring staff, I was told that the Commission for the Blind did not have enough money to operate the STEP program that year. The agency could neither pay the students' room and board nor hire the dorm counselors. I was told that I could work as a home teacher that summer. I was thankful to still have a job, but I wanted those forty-six blind students to work and be productive during the summer. What would they do while their sighted friends were going to sports events and working?

Terminating the program was a slap in the face for those kids. They needed adult role models, they needed to work, they needed to learn the skills of blindness, and they needed to learn to believe in themselves. I kept thinking and thinking about what I could do. DOL would pay the students' salaries and, after several phone calls, DOL agreed to pay for most of the job coaches. But I still needed money for room and board and for dorm counselors. By then, President Bill Clinton had appointed Fred Schroeder to be the commissioner of the Federal Rehabilitation Services Administration, and Arthur Schreiber (by that time, blind himself) was the new executive director of the Commission for the Blind.

Mr. Schreiber was a well-known and respected broad-caster, and he had managed the largest radio station in New Mexico. His career included serving as bureau chief for Westinghouse News. In the 1960s, he covered many of the most famous civil rights demonstrations, including the 1963 "I Have a Dream" speech that Martin Luther King Jr. delivered from the steps of the Lincoln Memorial. He also covered the 1965 Selma to Montgomery marches for voting rights.

Mr. Schreiber also served as the Westinghouse News White House correspondent during the Kennedy and Johnson administrations and traveled with the Beatles on their first United States cross-country tour in 1964. He was, to say the least, one of the most influential people in New Mexico at the time.

After much thought, it occurred to me that if Mr. Schreiber sent a letter to Dr. Richard Peck, president of the University of New Mexico, asking the university to partner with us on the STEP program, we might get some help. Arthur agreed, and I drafted the letter. After a couple of weeks, President Peck responded with an assurance that UNM would cover the cost of room and board for the students and would provide the dorm counselors. Area newspapers reported about the new partnership. We got right down to work.

The STEP coordinator job was very rewarding. Employers learned about the capabilities of blind people. Parents appreciated the change in their sons and daughters. Students gained positive self-esteem and a better understanding of themselves as blind people as they learned the importance of using the skills of blindness. The students—both those with additional disabilities and those without—did not learn to accept their limitations; they learned to challenge them.

• Chapter Twenty-Three •

RUNNING DREAMS

When I attended the school at the Orientation Center in Alamogordo, I ran on the track. Unfortunately, I ran too far and too fast in the beginning, and my knee started to hurt. I needed to be patient and build up my stamina gradually. But, because of that setback, I put my dream of running aside for a while.

I had other things to keep me busy. While working on my law and public administration degrees, I continued to work part-time for the Commission for the Blind. I also continued my active involvement in the NFB, including the National Association of Blind Students (the NFB's national student division). I traveled across the country to help organize new chapters, reorganize an affiliate, and start a new state student division. I had plenty to do, but I needed exercise and missed running.

During the summer of 1993, I was teaching a STEP student to get to the grocery store. He preferred to cook his meals on the weekends, rather than spending his money at restaurants. I encouraged him to eat out at least once per week, to practice social skills. As I coached him on crossing a parking lot, I told him to pick up his pace. I walked faster, with him a few steps behind me, to show him what I meant. Then, to my surprise, he ran to get ahead of me. His quick move caught me off guard, but it pleased me greatly to see a blind kid run with his white cane. After that experience, I resolved to start running again, using my cane.

I mentioned it to Fred Schroeder. He told me that in his prior work in the Albuquerque Public Schools, he taught little kids to use their canes, including running with them. Prior to Fred's innovation, traditional orientation and mobility instructors did not approve of giving canes to young children, because it seemed dangerous. They believed that youngsters weren't developmentally ready to use a cane.

I started jogging using my cane and gradually increased my stamina. After a few months, I felt ready for the next step. I dreamed of running full out again, like I had at the detective academy.

I asked a friend from my Bible study group to run with me. I tied one end of a rope around my left wrist and the other end around my running partner's right wrist. Unfortunately, this awkward arrangement didn't work. Either the rope didn't stay in place, or we couldn't establish a rhythm while running. Many times, my running partner ran too fast or too slow, and the rope would chafe our arms.

I needed to try something else. We came up with a new and simple system, using my cane. My running partner held my cane about forty inches away from the handle, while I held the handle. It worked well. But the first day, I could barely make it around the UNM track twice—only half a mile. My entire body ached. But I remained undeterred. I knew to expect pain in the beginning, but that if I continued, I'd get stronger. So I continued running twice per week.

Unfortunately, my friend's schedule did not match mine, so he quit. I found another running partner. That worked well for a couple of months, until he moved to another state. After that, I just walked and jogged some on my own. It changed my life. Exercise creates endorphins, which make us feel good and also relieve stress and pain. I felt healthier; plus, I simply enjoyed running. I had thought running while blind would be impossible. But I was changing my definition of impossible.

One afternoon, I got a call in my office. The man said, "My name is Ron Parks, and I was told to talk to you. Perhaps you could answer my question."

"Sure. How can I help you?"

He said, "I am a sighted person and a runner. I am looking for a running partner who can go out with me in the mornings. Do you know someone who might be interested?"

"As a matter of fact, yes! Actually, I am looking for someone to run with, but you know that I am blind, right?"

The man continued, "Well, yes, that's the reason I'm calling. My father was blind, and I knew that he could not run by himself."

We exchanged phone numbers and met at the track soon after. I explained that I could jog by myself, but I wanted to work with a partner to run faster and longer distances. Ron could only run early in the morning, which worked perfectly with my schedule.

Ron, a 52-year-old who ran between twenty and thirty miles per week, understood the joy of running outdoors. I showed him how I wanted to run with both of us holding the cane. He liked how it worked. He held my cane and stayed one step in front of me on my left. I held the handle of the cane and we took off. New running partners, we also quickly became good friends.

The first week, I could run only about a mile a day. By the third week, that mile became two, and by the second month, I easily ran three miles. I started out slowly, increasing my speed little by little. Ron timed us. I could run a nine-minute mile. Ron urged me to participate in a race, so I could meet more runners and make friends who could run with me.

With Ron's encouragement, we registered for my first race! I ran faster and faster each week. I enjoy running, have a competitive spirit, and am motivated to practice. I made a point of sleeping a full eight hours a day and eating a healthy diet.

By the time of the race, I had improved a great deal. I could run three miles in just over twenty-six minutes, or just a few seconds under nine minutes per mile. I had run much faster at the police academy, but I was not in that ultra-competitive environment anymore. I just wanted to have fun.

That first race filled me with elation! Passing other runners felt like a dream come true. Adrenaline rushed through me. I heard footsteps all around me and people cheering us on. Our success motivated us to practice for the next race, scheduled to take place on Father's Day.

At 5:00 a.m. the next day, as we stretched before our daily run, an older lady called out, "Hi, Ron."

Ron called back, "Hi, Lily. You did great yesterday."

I could hear the smile in Lily's voice. "So did you," she said.

As Ron and I ran, I asked him how old Lily was. She sounded over sixty to me. Ron said, "Oh, I think she is between seventy-two and seventy-five. Her son is a friend of mine, and he also likes to run."

Ron and I had run hard the previous day, so we jogged at an easy pace, making conversation easy. I kept thinking about Lily being over seventy and running. I was impressed.

I asked Ron, "What was Lily's time yesterday?"

"I don't know." Ron seemed surprised by my question. "Why don't we ask her? She just got back from running and is stretching."

I was taken aback. She just got back from running, too?

"Hey Lily, what was your time yesterday?" Ron asked.

"Oh, I did it in twenty-five minutes," Lily said breezily.

I felt awed by this 72-year-old woman who could run three miles in twenty-five minutes when it took me more than twenty-six minutes to go the same distance! And I was only in my late twenties.

As Ron and Lily talked, I thought about the disparity in our ages and running abilities. Who was this woman? Ron commented later, "Don't worry, Carlos. You are a natural runner and, with a few more weeks of practice, you will run as fast as Lily."

I thought about Ron's words. I knew that I would not be satisfied running as fast as Lily. I wanted to run faster. I wanted to beat her! I didn't dwell on it, but I didn't miss any of my early morning running sessions either.

Ron introduced me to a new friend, Charlie Otero. Charlie and Ron took turns running with me. Two months later, I was ready for my next challenge: to run faster than Lily.

I could now run three miles in just under twenty-five minutes and felt determined to do my best in that next race. I felt focused, much like the time I took the exam to be accepted into the detective academy. I just hoped that Lily would also be in the race.

Early on the morning of the race, I was on the mark ready to go, determined to run faster than Lily, my friendly running rival. The announcer shouted through his megaphone to start, and we took off. A light breeze provided some relief from the bright, hot sun. Due to the dry air in Albuquerque, the course included two water stations, but I didn't want to stop. I was determined to make this my best time ever!

I heard steady, measured footsteps all around me, people cheering, and runners talking as they ran. As the race progressed, the field of runners spread out. I felt great, but I could only think of beating Lily! Was she ahead of me? Behind me? Gaining on me?

Ron let me know when we reached the first milepost, and we picked up the pace, passing more and more people. I breathed deeply, inhaling and exhaling rhythmically, taking long, strong strides, concentrating intently.

Ron asked if I wanted to stop for water, but I declined. We went on, maintaining a consistent speed and passing more and more people.

At the second milepost, I asked Ron, "Hey, do you see Lily?"

The sound of runners around me changed as Ron shifted his position to look behind and ahead of us.

"She's around twenty yards ahead," he said. I could tell he was trying not to laugh.

I took a deep breath and pushed the cane forward to let Ron know that I wanted to run faster. We picked up our pace and, when we got to the fourth kilometer, or around 200 yards into the last mile, I asked again for Lily's whereabouts.

This time, Ron didn't need to look around. He knew I was looking for Lily. "She is three or four yards in front of us. Hey, you really want to pass her?" he said, sounding amused, even as he began to pick up the pace.

My thoughts drifted back twelve years to a one-mile race, required as part of the examination for acceptance into the Peruvian Army School of Officers. It felt like déjà vu! After the officer in charge gave the command to start, twenty young, fit candidates began to run. As we ran, dust trailed after us like a cloud. Twenty candidates, breathing hard as we ran faster and faster, pounded around the dirt track. We had trained for this important test, knowing that only the best would be accepted.

We ran four times around the track. After the first round, I accelerated, passing some candidates and moving ahead little by little.

"Carlos, concentrate. Look ahead. Inhale deeply through your nose. Exhale through your mouth. Do your best!" I thought as I ran. After 500 meters, I had worked my way into third place. Focused and full of determination, I lengthened my stride as I entered the last 400 meters of the race. I pushed myself to go faster and faster. Only one runner strode ahead of me, and I was intent on passing him.

The lead runner blocked my way to prevent me from passing, so I stayed one step behind. With 120 meters to go, we both dug in, determined to win. Into the last turn of the race, with one hundred meters left, sprinting as fast as I could, I drew next to him before he could block me again. We raced side by side, hearing each other breathe, matching each other step for step. Looking straight ahead and running even harder, I pulled a little ahead. Only seventy meters to go. The air streamed past my face as I pushed myself to run faster. My legs and lungs burned, but I kept on going. Pain didn't matter. Twenty meters, ten, five. I crossed the finish line.

Back to the present, I heard the crowd excitedly cheering, "good job, good job, yeah!" I beat Lily! I felt great, and my chest swelled with pride!

Ron walked us to one side as I struggled to catch my breath. I continued gasping for air when Lily came up just a few seconds after we finished. She congratulated me. She seemed not tired at all! I still couldn't breathe and couldn't even reply.

"Carlos, you did great. Good job," Lily said, in a motherly way, patting my shoulder. I felt a little patronized, but I smiled as I fought to catch my breath.

As I struggled to recover, the announcer called the runners of the ten-kilometer race to get ready. Ron and Lily went to get into position. I could not believe it! Lily had just been warming up! I felt thoroughly demoralized. Upon reflection, I concluded that I should be happy to have improved my speed. After all, I had many more years to run. My new friend and role model, Lily, had just taught me that.

These days, I have running dreams, but they've changed. The dark dreams of being stuck or unable to move are gone. In my new dream, the colors around me are vivid in the bright sunlight. I run easily, feeling the wind on my face. My legs feel powerful, and I flow along as if I'm flying. Nothing is holding me back, and I'm free.

• Epilogue •

On a bright, sunny morning in May 1997, I graduated from the University of New Mexico (UNM) with a juris doctorate and a master's in public administration. The commencement ceremony took place on a golf course behind the UNM School of Law, with the Sandia Mountains rising majestically in the background.

Cati, our two young children, and my mother were there as I went forward to receive my diploma. My brothers and sisters from Germany and Peru also came, as well as cousins from both Virginia and California. My great friend and mentor, Fred Schroeder, came all the way from Washington, DC, to be with me on this very special day in my life. In fact, Fred's brother, Steve, hosted a delightful graduation party for me at his house.

Graduating with a law degree and master's degree was a major achievement, and the day was one of the happiest of my life. I felt like everything was working out just as I hoped. After much hard work and perseverance, I was ready to move on.

At that time, according to the US Immigration and Naturalization Service (INS), under the terms of my J-1 visa, I could extend my stay if I secured "practical training" in my area of studies. In other words, I could do legal research in a law firm or work for a governmental agency in a position related to public administration. I was still working part time for the New Mexico Commission for the Blind under the practical training authority of the J-1 student visa, but I needed to find a permanent job.

My J-1 visa would expire a year and a half later, at the end of December 1998. After that, to stay in the United States, I would need to secure an H-1 temporary work visa. To qualify for that visa, I needed a job contract with a firm or agency. A condition of the temporary work visa was that the immigrant does not take a job from a qualified American citizen. Assuming I remained employed, the H-1 visa would enable me to stay and work in the US until my turn came with the INS to process my application for residency under my mother's visa.

Because of the restriction that my employment does not take a job from a qualified American, I could not find a potential employer who could or would offer me a contract. I had a sinking feeling—the same one I felt when I needed a sponsor—that I might not be able to stay in America. The employment prospects in Peru were not bright either. Even though terrorism had mostly been eradicated, the economic situation was still difficult and even harder for blind people.

One morning in May, I was in my office working while listening to the news about the death of Frank Sinatra when my phone rang.

"This is Dr. Pearl Van Zandt, director of Nebraska Services for the Visually Impaired. I have a position to fill, and Dr. Schroeder recommended you for the job."

"Can you tell me about the job and its duties?" I hardly

dared allow myself to think that this might be the answer to my staying in America.

"I am looking for a deputy director for Vocational Rehabilitation Services, someone who can help me transform the agency's culture to increase job placements. Are you interested?" Dr. Van Zandt asked.

"Yes. That is just the kind of job I am looking for. I feel confident that I can meet your expectations." This opportunity sounded really good.

"Okay, good. Well, today is the deadline to apply. Can you give me your fax number? I will send you the application as soon as we hang up. Can you fill it out and fax it back to me today?"

I immediately filled out and returned my application. Two weeks later, I had a telephone interview with Dr. Van Zandt; Bob Deaton, deputy director of Independent Living Services; and Joyce Van Patten, transition coordinator. The day after the interview, Dr. Van Zandt called me and asked me to come to Nebraska for a face-to-face follow-up interview with the field supervisors and the training center supervisor.

In preparation for the interview, I researched the philosophy of Nebraska Services for the Visually Impaired (SVI) and its relationship with its consumers. Impressed by what I discovered, I thought it would be a great place to work. After the follow-up interview, I was offered the position of deputy director of Vocational Rehabilitation Services, and I accepted. I was set. My J-1 visa would not expire until the end of the year, which gave me plenty of time to apply for the H-1 temporary work visa.

At the end of July 1998, Cati, our two children, and I moved to Lincoln, Nebraska. Cati said most of the people in Lincoln were Caucasian. She saw few Hispanic, Black, or Native American people—quite different from the varied cultures represented in New Mexico.

I learned later that some of the most prominent National Federation of the Blind (NFB) blindness professionals had worked in Nebraska, including some of my favorite people—the Boones and Fred Schroeder.

Since I was working under my J-1 student visa and using the practical training option to stay in the country after graduation, I needed to get the paperwork done and sent in before it expired in December. I called INS and was told that the process would take no more than three months. That meant that I had until the end of September to submit the documentation. Never one to wait until the last minute, I sent in the required documentation in the middle of August.

The end of December came, but no visa arrived. INS assured me that, as long as I had sent in my paperwork on time, I was legally in the US. However, there was one problem, and it was a big one. I could not work or get governmental assistance until I had the H-1 temporary work visa. That meant that my salary stopped, and we were left waiting. Cati and I were full of anxiety, as day after day went by and no visa came in the mail. With a four-year-old and a two-year-old to care for, what little savings we had dwindled quickly. The local Catholic church helped with food and donations, and the Lincoln Action Program paid our rent and utilities for one month.

Even though I was no longer being paid, I went to work every day and performed my duties conscientiously. But, truth be told, I was distracted by our stressful financial situation and worried about when relief might come.

One day, when I checked my mailbox to see if my visa had arrived, I found an envelope and brought it back to my office. When my reader opened it, she discovered that it contained $1,300. I learned later that an employee had organized a collection. The money helped pay rent, some overdue bills, and food for another month. It also made me realize how privileged I was to work with such generous people.

The end of January arrived and still no H-1 visa. I kept praying for the work visa to get to me or for any financial help in the meantime. Then, a leader of the NFB called and said he heard about my financial problems and the delay in getting my work visa. He said he would send me a few thousand dollars to help us get by. He made me promise not to tell anyone. His only condition was that I must attend the NFB Washington seminar, something I had been doing every year since 1992. At the Washington seminar, blind people from around the country talk with their representatives and senators to educate them about legislation that would promote greater independence, better education, and equal employment opportunities for blind children and adults. Once again, the NFB stepped in to help me. I could not stop thinking about how many times this valuable organization, with its great, dedicated leaders, continued to come through for blind people.

Finally, in the middle of April, my H-1 temporary work visa arrived. I met with a human resources representative from the Nebraska Department of Health and Human Services (the umbrella agency administering SVI). I was there to get my salary reinstated under my new H-1 visa. The human resources representative told me that, even though I had not been paid since December, the State had been paying my health insurance and making my retirement payments. The representative told me that I had to pay back three-and-a-half months of contributions. Not an easy prospect given our situation. Once again, I remembered that life can play tricks on us by presenting us with an unexpected turn of events. I had to be ready to face life's challenges, whatever they might be, especially with a young family to support.

At that time, I was serving on the NFB Scholarship Committee. In April 1998, at the scholarship committee meeting in Baltimore, Dr. Jernigan talked with us. Dr. Kenneth

Jernigan was the previous longtime president of the NFB. He was a builder, a teacher, and a great inspirational leader. He had lung cancer, which made his voice very weak. One evening after dinner, a few of us stood in the hallway near the reception desk talking about the idea of building a new building, a National Institute for the Blind, run by the blind. When everyone else had drifted away, and we were alone, I asked him, "Dr. Jernigan, do you think we will be able to raise $15 million to build the Institute? We are talking about a lot of money."

Although his voice was weak, his message was strong. He pounded the tip of his cane on the floor as he spoke. "Oh, yes, Carlos, we will raise the money. I have no doubt about it," he said with his customary conviction, purpose, and resolve.

Once again, I learned an important lesson. Dr. Jernigan was a man who knew he had only a few months to live and yet he was still building for the next generation of the blind. He dared to write a different story about the blind; he dared to challenge the blind to work collectively for a brighter future; and he dared to confront society with the truth about blindness. In 1958, he became the director of the Iowa Commission for the Blind and developed it into a model state program with a revolutionary new approach to training blind people. It was this program on which the New Mexico and Nebraska programs are based.

At the end of 1999, I was granted temporary residency under my mother's immigration status. She was already a US resident, so under "family reunification" she was able to sponsor me for immigration to the United States. One year later, I could apply for permanent residency. A year after that, I could apply for citizenship. This was another important milestone, beginning a long and complicated process that moved very slowly.

When George W. Bush was elected president, leaders of

the NFB approached me as a potential candidate for nomination for US assistant secretary of labor. One of the first questions they asked dealt with my US citizenship. Because I answered, "No, I'm not a citizen," my name was never submitted for President Bush's consideration.

I became a US citizen in 2003. Citizenship gave me more pride and confidence. I remember the federal judge who conducted the citizenship ceremony saying something like, "Welcome to the United States of America. We are a great country because we are made of immigrants like you. Let's continue building a free and diverse country."

I received job offers from around the country. It was gratifying but overwhelming. A short time earlier, I could not apply for jobs because of my immigration status. Now I was being offered jobs to head agencies for the blind.

In 2001, President Bush appointed Joanne Wilson (a blind woman and a longtime leader in the NFB), to be the commissioner of the Rehabilitation Services Administration (RSA), the position Dr. Schroeder held under President Clinton. Two years later, Joanne encouraged me to apply to head RSA's Division of Services for the Blind. It was one of the highest-level positions at RSA. Joe Cordova had held the job but was leaving to become the RSA Regional Commissioner for regions V and VII. It sounded like a dream job, and I prepared for the interview. I asked Joe Cordova to tell me the good and bad about the position. He told me the disadvantage was that he did not have much contact with blind consumers, something he missed. However, state administrators called him for guidance, and he had a great impact on services for the blind around the country.

In 2003, when Joanne Wilson offered me the job, I immediately accepted. I stepped down as president of the NFBN and also resigned from the NFB National Board of Directors to avoid any appearance of a conflict of interest. President Bush just needed to approve the appointment. A few weeks after I was offered the job, the president announced that, because of the conflict in the Middle East and the need to save money, all top federal positions had been frozen, so I didn't get the job. That was probably just as well. In 2005, the position was eliminated, along with the RSA regional offices.

Staying in Lincoln worked out well. Cati liked it and did not want to leave. It was big enough to have all the advantages of a big city without all the big city problems. She was happy that the RSA job offer fell through. She helped me think less about myself and my career and more about us as a family and the future of our children. She liked the school the kids were in and the people she worked with. Bottom line? Cati simply didn't want to uproot the family. I eventually came around to her way of thinking and started telling people who called with job offers that I was not available. I was going to stay in Nebraska. After all, I enjoyed NCBVI—both the people who worked there and the consumers we served. With that decided, Cati and I purchased a home in Lincoln.

For now, I will continue giving my best in our beloved Nebraska. But in my present running dreams, I'm always pressing toward a horizon glowing with even greater empowerments for people with disabilities. Refusing to be held back, we, too, have running dreams. Federal agencies are uniquely situated to turn bigger dreams into fulfilling realities. So, if an opening to help lead a key federal agency presents itself, I think of submitting my name. I recall Dr. Maurer's reminder of Seneca's definition of 'luck': "When Preparation Meets Opportunity." Just, perhaps, I could get 'lucky'!

As Deputy Director of the Commission, I attended meetings about the employment of blind and other disabled people. One training I attended concerned the employment of people with multiple disabilities, especially those with intellectual and developmental disabilities. The training reinforced my philosophy about services for the blind, including those who had additional disabilities. The keynote speaker was a father of a young man with a developmental disability who had been trained to operate a restaurant dishwasher. His son started and failed in a number of restaurant dishwashing jobs before he achieved success. When the dad asked the son why he did a good job at the last restaurant and not at the previous ones where the dishwashing machines were the same, the son had a simple and profound answer, "Because at this place they like me."

That is what it takes to work with people with disabilities. Like anyone else, people with disabilities want to be accepted and treated with respect. As rehabilitation professionals, we need to open our hearts, listen to what is being said, and respond with genuine concern and compassion. I saw these qualities in Joe Cordova, Dr. Schroeder, Dr. Maurer, and in many others who have been successful in working with blind people. It is the approach I used when I coordinated the STEP program in New Mexico, and it is the approach I continue to use at NCBVI.

Early in June 2017, Dr. Van Zandt announced her retirement as executive director of NCBVI, effective on July 9. The board of commissioners named me interim director while they conducted a national search. I applied for the position, but I must confess that, even though I knew I qualified for the job and was prepared to run one of the finest agencies in the country, I thought that being an immigrant and having a heavy accent would count against me. I didn't take anything for granted. I tried to imagine myself in the position of a commissioner interviewing an applicant to anticipate the kinds of questions that might be asked. Then I spent several nights writing and rewriting my answers in response to those questions.

The commission board determined that I was the most

qualified applicant and, on August 18, 2017, I was offered the position of NCBVI executive director.

Many of the staff and consumers supported my application, but some did not. It's like my father once said, "The more successful you are, the more enemies you make." I think of these words often, particularly when I am faced with tough decisions, knowing that some people will be unhappy with me no matter what I do. I learned a long time ago to stay focused and think about solutions. I listen to what people have to say and make the decisions that need to be made, always keeping in mind the mission of the agency. One thing I have learned from my struggles is that the greater the challenge, the greater the sense of accomplishment and joy when success is realized.

I have traveled both within the US and abroad promoting a positive philosophy of blindness and life in general. I have shared my personal story of growing up poor in Peru, getting into the detective academy, becoming blind, struggling to survive as a blind person in Peru, coming to America with few resources and not knowing English, and what it has taken to reach my dreams, including how blindness training has changed my life and can do the same for others. On many occasions, after I have finished speaking, people have come up to me wanting to know more about me and my life. Many were parents of blind children, who were inspired by my story and what it might mean for their children. Spouses of blind people and blind people themselves said that my story motivated them to change their lives in positive ways.

I realized that I was touching the lives of others in the same profound way Dr. Schroeder, Dr. Maurer, and others had touched mine.

Many people urged me to write a book. At first, I didn't take the idea seriously. I knew plenty of blind people were doing the same things I was doing and more. Still, people continued telling me to write it, especially sighted people.

They said my story was amazing, and it needed to be told.

I finally decided to write this book, not because I think I am amazing or extraordinary or that others should believe that I am, but just the opposite. Extraordinary events have occurred in my life, but I am just a regular guy who was fortunate enough to get the proper training, hang around positive people, and take advantage of opportunities that presented themselves.

On July 23, 2017, I officially presented my book and spoke at the Feria Internacional del Libro Lima (Lima International Book Fair). The Lima International Book Fair is held annually and attracts more than half a million people. All of my family and friends were there to hear me speak. It was another powerful milestone in my life and inspired me to start working on the English version of my book. This book is a little different from the Spanish version, though.

I have been privileged to work with fine people like Dr. Schroeder, Joe Cordova, Barbara Loos, Dr. Van Zandt, Mark Bulger, Mike Hansen, Bob Deaton, Carol Jenkins, Connie Daly, Nancy Flearl, and many others. They also challenged me, as they were constantly checking my pulse. I believe that my two worlds have fused—Peru, where I grew up, and America, where I continue to grow. Ranging backward in time to understand my roots helps me look forward to anticipate future consequences. I want to always remember where I came from, because it reinvigorates my soul. Every year, I visit Peru, reconnecting with friends from my neighborhood, their parents, friends from primary and secondary school, and friends from the National Police.

I continue to be actively involved in the National Federation of the Blind. Each year, I attend federation state and national conventions. My involvement renews my commitment to serving blind people and reminds me that, as a blind person, I can do far more than society assumes.

Throughout the course of my life, during the most difficult times, I noticed that spirit, mind, and body synchronize so we can overcome those obstacles. Also, when times were desperate, I had faith and therefore received help when I needed it most. I believe that helping others is one of the best ways to change the world. If all of us make the effort to help others when we can, the world will be a different and better place.

As I reflect on events in my life, I realize that becoming blind did not change me. Blindness presented challenges that I had to deal with, for sure, but the values and personal qualities acquired over a lifetime were what determined how I managed adversity. This journey did not change the essence of my principles but amplified it.

I am still the executive director of the Nebraska Commission for the Blind and Visually Impaired. My children, Macaulan, Carlos, Sheyannah, and Doris, are grown and have graduated from college. Cati works at The Hub-Central Access for Young Adults providing academic and other support to high school students at high risk of dropping out. Thus far, my journey has been challenging, but joyful.

These days, I can't help but reflect upon how my tormenting nightmares became uplifting, running dreams, shimmering with vivid colors. My heart is filled with good dreams for every reader of this book—especially those who may be in a hard place right now, whether struggling with a disability or intimidated by life's painful hurdles. My sleeping dreams stopped plaguing me with feeling stuck, unable to move. The exhilarating wind on my face, my legs feeling powerful, I was running free in the next beckoning lap of the race. For every running dreamer, I wish for you the strength and faith to overcome obstacles. May you experience God's presence; the joy of the next, new, independent step; growth in love and loyalties; and an ever-expanding circle of friends who help one another. If *Running Dreams* inspires you, my readers, to stay steady, to overcome hurdles, to keep running, your triumphs will enrich my dreams.

• Acknowledgements •

I would not be able to write this book without the support of talented friends who motivated me and helped me throughout the writing process.

I am grateful to Bob Deaton who helped me put many of my thoughts into a compelling narrative, and to Dr. Fredric K. Schroeder who did the first editing and gave me honest feedback; to Jeff Altman, who also helped me put in words the first part of this book; to Barbara Loos and Dan Frye who took their time to proofread this narrative; To Carolina Mejía, who worked as an assistant throughout the writing process; and, finally, to the excellent editorial team from Atmosphere Press.

To Joe Cordova who was my first mentor in America and provided me moral support.

To Eileen Rivera Ley, who since she met me, believed in my capabilities, and connected me with other blind role models.

To my brothers and sisters, who are always supporting each other and willing to help, no matter what.

To my wife and children, who gave me total support from the beginning and provided their honest feedback throughout the writing process.

About Atmosphere Press

Atmosphere Press is an independent, full-service publisher for excellent books in all genres and for all audiences. Learn more about what we do at atmospherepress.com.

We encourage you to check out some of Atmosphere's latest releases, which are available at Amazon.com and via order from your local bookstore:

The Great Unfixables, by Neil Taylor

Soused at the Manor House, by Brian Crawford

Portal or Hole: Meditations on Art, Religion, Race And The Pandemic, by Pamela M. Connell

A Walk Through the Wilderness, by Dan Conger

The House at 104: Memoir of a Childhood, by Anne Hegnauer

A Short History of Newton Hall, Chester, by Chris Fozzard

Serial Love: When Happily Ever After... Isn't, by Kathy Kay

Sit-Ins, Drive-Ins and Uncle Sam, by Bill Slawter

Black Water and Tulips, by Sara Mansfield Taber

Ghosted: Dating & Other Paramoural Experiences, by Jana Eisenstein

Walking with Fay: My Mother's Uncharted Path into Dementia, by Carolyn Testa

FLAWED HOUSES of FOUR SEASONS, by James Morris

Word for New Weddings, by David Glusker and Thom Blackstone

It's Really All about Collaboration and Creativity! A Textbook and Self-Study Guide for the Instrumental Music Ensemble Conductor, by John F. Colson

A Life of Obstructions, by Rob Penfield

• About the Author •

PHOTO BY SABRINA RAINS

Carlos R. Serván, born and raised in Peru, immigrated to the USA in 1989, shortly after losing his vision and right hand in a grenade explosion while a cadet at the detective academy. Carlos is a passionate, motivational speaker and international disability rights advocate. His first book—in Spanish—was the second-best seller, memoir category, at the International Book Fair in Lima.

He earned his MPA and JD from the University of New Mexico and presently directs the Nebraska Commission for the Blind. Carlos Serván resides in Lincoln, Nebraska, with his wife. Devoted to fitness, he is a zealous runner.